Soul
SALT

ISBN (paperback) 979-8-9851902-5-0
ISBN (ebook) 979-8-9851902-4-3
Library of Congress Control Number: 2023932985

Lead Editor: Kevin Mullani
Editor: Hayden Seder
Illustrator: Erin Blutt

Cover & Interior Design: Innovator Press
www.InnovatorPress.com

Printed in the United States

ADVANCE PRAISE

"I've known Lyn for years, as a colleague, coach, and friend. Creating your own Soul Salt Map offers illuminating insights into how Lyn coaches, and more importantly, how they truly live. Listen carefully, their lessons will speak to your soul."

—Marva Sadler
COO, Coaching.com

"You know a book is exceptional when you feel relief upon discovering it. Lyn's invitation is so authentic and their technique so insightful and comprehensive. It's clear you're being guided by a master coach and sage. Soul Salt is a literary feat of co-elevation."

—Sunni Brown
Social Entrepreneur and Bestselling Author

"I have been fortunate to have Lyn as a mentor in my career as well as coach our team of sales executives in bringing their best selves forward with confidence. I'm excited that everyone can now experience what we have learned—read Soul Salt, do the exercises, and be the person that is living your truth."

—Judy Copier
Market President, iHeart Media

"Soul Salt is a LIFELINE. This book belongs on the bookshelf of every single person who embraces a growth mindset and is interested in growth and development—personally, spiritually and professionally."

—Shannon Judge
Founder/Head Coach, Vitality Coaching & Wellness

"*Every conversation I've had with Lyn has formed an inflection point in my life, bolstered my confidence, and helped me see my situation with new eyes. Soul Salt will give you that same experience. As a Master Coach, Lyn offers practical exercises and accessible, evidence-based guidance to help you recognize your values, then align your life and career with them. With crisp, direct prose and a no-nonsense, but supremely compassionate approach, Lyn will help you understand that ultimately you are your own guide.*"

—Dr. Jennifer Raff
NYT Bestselling Author, *Origin: A Genetic History of the Americas*
Affiliate Faculty, Indigenous Studies, Assoc. Prof. and Director
of Graduate Studies, Anthropology, University of Kansas

"*Many experts talk about purpose as the key to happiness, but few can tell you how to actually find it. Lyn can—and shares all the tools in this astonishingly practical field guide. I can't wait to share this book with everyone I know who, like me in midlife, is still searching for direction and meaning.*"

—Johanna Nastor
Director of Operations, Digital Commerce Partners

"*I knew I was in good hands when Lyn supported me to find deeper levels of my personal and professional identity. By working through these exercises you can receive the same tools and stay at the top of your game. You are sure to find clarity and affirmation within the pages of Soul Salt.*"

—Sam Villa
Co-Founder & Chief Creative Officer
The Sam Villa Company | Allvus LLC

Soul SALT

Your Personal Field Guide to
Confidence, Purpose, and Fulfillment

LYN CHRISTIAN

INNOVATOR
PRESS
Boise, Idaho

CONTENTS

Learning to trust your soul ... it lies in opposition to looking to others for life purpose and personal teaching ... and it waits patiently for us each day, quietly calling us back home.

Your soul knows the geography of your destiny. Your soul alone has the map of your future, therefore, you can trust this indirect and oblique side of yourself. If you do, it will take you where you need to go. But more important, it will teach you a kindness of rhythm in your journey.

—John O Donohue

by Dr. Marshall Goldsmith

As an Executive Coach for the last 40 years, my mission has been to help successful people get even better. Working with leaders in a variety of industries around the world, I've had the opportunity to work with many people at the top of their careers and fields and unlock their highest potential with them. Many of my clients expect for the most value in our coaching to come from strategical planning and the work we conduct for their professional advancement. However, the most critical part of this coaching is often working on the whole person and digging into the balance and fulfillment of both their personal and professional life.

I've found that many of my clients and people I meet have deep regrets about the choices they'd made in their personal lives that affect how they handle current stressors and decisions. In writing my latest book, *The Earned Life*, I talk about a powerful practice I work on with my clients called The Every Breath Paradigm.

The philosophy behind this is that each and every breath you take is a "new you." The new person is only responsible for the actions, words, and decisions in this breath, right now. This means that you are no longer the person who made the decisions of your past, nor the person who will make any decisions in the future. While you can appreciate that your past selves have helped shape you and make you the person who is here today, you can separate yourself from the guilt and regrets you may hold on to, as you are not the same person who made those decisions. They gave you the gift of the life and love you have, but this separation allows you to remove yourself from the pain of being connected to them. Rather, you can forgive these past versions of yourself. You can let go of what they may hold on to, and instead focus on this next breath and being the best version of yourself to become another gift for a future breath. This practice has been revolutionary for my clients that enjoy the freedom of being able to move forward and make the choices they want to in this moment and live in the present without the burdens of their past.

Soul Salt is all about finding your worth, purpose, and leading the life you desire—starting today! This book will teach you to look critically and deeply at your life to find your true passions and identity. Lyn Christian's profound research and insights in this area will help you to live your truth and find meaning for your life. Whether you're ready for a career change, feeling burnout, or discovering that the purpose you've been living for hasn't been something you've chosen for yourself, this is the book for you.

Take a deep breath in. This is a new you. This is a you that is ready to take control of your life and happiness that starts here.

Dr. Marshall Goldsmith is the *Thinkers50* #1 Executive Coach and New York Times bestselling author of *The Earned Life*, *Triggers*, and *What Got You Here Won't Get You There*.

INTRODUCTION

You have just been told you have three months to live. I could ask what you will do with your final weeks, but I'm not interested in how you spend your remaining time. What I want to know, and what I want you to consider, is whether or not you have regrets. What did you do, or not do, with the majority of the time you had, and, did you live a confident, purpose-filled, joyful life?

If not, what would you do differently if you could go back in time?

Bronnie Ware had the same curiosity but was in a position to actually find out. She worked in palliative care where she had the privilege to help seriously ill patients with only three to twelve weeks to live. She asked her patients questions similar to those above, then published a book titled, *The Top Five Regrets of the Dying*. Based on her experiences she discovered there were five common themes that turned up again and again in the answers she gathered. Number one on that list was:

> *I wish I'd had the courage to live a life true to myself, not the life others expected of me.*[1]

1

I pray to all that is good that you have more than three months left to live. I also hope that you are not full of regrets ... but you may be. Either way, I know you were drawn to this book because something is *off*, whether you are aware of it or not. I know you have a deeper calling to something inside that needs to be free. Something that will allow you to live the rest of your life with the confidence, purpose, and fulfillment that you don't have right now. I also know from helping thousands of clients how rare it is for someone to truly know who they are. Even if they know, it's even more rare that they actively co-create their life based upon that truth.

PERSONAL BELIEFS OR PROGRAMS?

How many of your personal beliefs and behaviors do you think you chose on your own?

What if I told you that 95% of our beliefs and behaviors are hardwired into our subconscious by age seven?[2] Think about that for a second. How many deep conversations did you have before the age of seven about what was genuinely important to you, how you wanted to design your life, and what things were imperative to your happiness? I'm guessing exactly zero!

95% of our beliefs and behaviors are hardwired into our subconscious by age seven...

Instead, you operated on a system where you wanted to please your parents, teachers, and other authority figures. You picked up on their words, tone of voice, and actions, which shaped your behaviors to fit in, or make them happy. Consequently, you invented ingenious ways to stuff down parts of your own identity that bubbled up in order to be "safe" around adults. You unwittingly compromised who you truly were.

Additionally, common interactions generated social cues that confirmed you needed to adapt to what others thought. Here are some basic examples:

Child: "I'm scared!"

Adult: "Don't be silly, there's nothing to be afraid of."

Resultant Belief: I'm not supposed to feel what I'm feeling.

Child: "I really love when we go to the local amusement park. Can we visit Disneyland someday?"

Adult: "Be thankful for what you have and stop daydreaming."

Resultant Belief: It's not safe to say what I really want.

Child: "I love drawing. I want to grow up to be an artist."

Adult: With a furrowed brow, "Artist!? Nobody makes a good living as an artist."

Resultant Belief: Forget about joy and fulfillment at work. Be practical instead.

It's a shame when this happens to a little person. And it even happens in the *best* of situations. Your parents and other adults were only acting in what they thought were your best interests. Unfortunately, there is no required class that teaches adults how to nurture a child's true self. Most parents learned what they know from their parents, and they learned from their parents before them. So, unless they've read a book like this one, chances are good you've experienced similar interactions to the scenarios above.

My first memory of suppressing who I knew myself to be was at age five. I found myself in a nose-to-nose shouting match with my paternal grandmother who insisted that I, "Take off those jeans, put on a dress, and act like a young lady." To which I shouted back, "I'm not a girl. I won't ever be a lady!"

I was full of fight and indignation because I felt misunderstood and that my grandmother was blind to the individual I knew I truly was. Yet, when you are the child in a crowd of adults, you lose more of these battles than you win. So, off went the jeans, on went the dress, and a disconnection with who I am began.

The weight of someone's opinions and beliefs who I saw as an authority, along with their assumed position of being right, pressed me into conformity. As years passed, like anything that gets repeated many times, it became easier and easier to set myself aside and adopt principles, values, beliefs, and opinions that were not actually mine.

Fast-forward to age 33 and the buildup of conformity hit a crescendo. I woke up to the fact that I was deeply unhappy in a relationship that no longer worked and my life didn't reflect my authentic nature and strength. Scores of people tried to intervene and tell me what I *ought* to be doing, *should* be doing, and *could* be doing. Fortunately, one or two brave souls took me under their wing and showed me how they had flown away from conformity and into the arms of personal truth. This awakened a deep desire to trust what was now hidden within my own identity—so the excavation began.

I dug in, took notes, experimented, and learned to speak the language of my own thoughts, feelings, and motivations. I eventually rediscovered, revealed, and in many cases recovered myself from what had become a fearful, unsatisfying life. I have continued to unearth and brush off pieces hiding my buried identity. The journey took time, yet along the way I noticed that I was happier, healthier, more confident, and more productive than I'd ever been.

I'm proud to finally say that I earn a living and live a life based around the truth of who I am. And, because the processes and strategies I utilized worked so well for me, others took notice. They wanted what I uncovered—the secret source of living as their most authentic self—which I will share with you in the pages ahead.

DO THE WORK, OR STAY DISCONNECTED?

The problem is, there is still an original *you* deep inside that wants to come out and be true to itself. The voice may be quieter, and you may be quicker to dismiss it, but it is definitely still there. Even if you *think* you know who you are and what you want from life, most of the information you need was stripped out or watered down well before you could use it. Eventually, you wake up feeling stuck, lost, off-purpose, and/or ready for a drastic shift, but don't know why, or what to do about it.

Does that sound familiar?

There is still an original you deep inside that wants to come out and be true to itself.

It's pretty evident what happens when we get disconnected from the origins of self that make us who we are. See if any of these resonate with you:

- Most of us belong to, and have adopted principles of, systems that were imposed on us instead of finding systems that contain principles which resonate with those buried within our hearts.

- As much as 80% of the workforce goes to work using pseudo-strengths (things we are good at but find no joy in doing) instead of superpowers (things we are extremely good at and find invigorating to perform).

- We try to meet the needs of others rather than get our own shit together first.

- We inadvertently mold ourselves into "practical" people who figure things out in our heads, but stay disconnected from our dreams, aspirations, and possibilities.

- We bow down to a paycheck while our soul hungers to sink its teeth into purpose and meaning.

- We jump through hoops earning grades, labels, and bonuses, but forget to create and use metrics that measure soul-satisfying success.

And where does all of this leave us? Mostly living a life that isn't really the life we wanted to live—going to work for a paycheck instead of serving a meaningful purpose, and reacting to life instead of designing the life we actually desire.

The pandemic of 2020 was the latest catalyst to cause large numbers of workers to examine their careers and reevaluate if their current professional trajectory aligns with what they want. Many decided it wasn't, which resulted in the *great resignation*—downsizing, reinventing careers, and starting over. They are now seeking the kinds of answers, wisdom, and guidance that only come when we stop and dig deep into the very salt of one's soul.

WHAT IS SOUL SALT?

All too often, we only hear about the negative side of salt. However, salt plays a crucial role in maintaining the health of the body. Saline is required to support healthy brain function and is in the fluids that support your eyes. Saline is also found in amniotic fluid, which supported your body from the earliest stages of life. Sodium is essential for nerve and muscle function and is involved in the regulation of fluids in the body.[3] Additionally, sodium plays a major role in the body's control of blood volume.[4] Blood is arguably one of the most important elements that continuously delivers life-giving oxygen and nutrients to every part of the body. Similarly, our soul requires that we access and utilize life-giving, personal attributes to live with confidence, purpose, and fulfillment.

History is also dotted with references measuring one's worth related to salt. Soldiers in the Roman army were sometimes paid with salt. Their monthly allowance was called *salarium*—*sal* being the Latin word for salt.[5] It is believed that this is also the origin of the phrase, "worth his salt," which essentially means, worth one's pay. The modern word *salary* derives from the Latin word salarium as well.[6]

As a master coach, I constantly help people uncover the infallible elements that, when mapped and used for guidance, reveal their worth to themselves and to the world. When these elements are revealed, my clients have increased their sense of self, raised their level of confidence, improved connection, and created a path to purpose and personal fulfillment. I call these unique and personal elements the salt of the soul, or Soul Salt.

I help people uncover the infallible elements that, when mapped and used for guidance, reveal their worth to themselves and to the world.

ARE YOU A GOOD FIT FOR THIS BOOK?

I refer to Soul Salt as the valuable aspects of you that brings your worth forward. But, here's the deal—I've been coaching for decades now and I've yet to encounter a single client who had a full, competent handle on their own worth.

There are some who tell me right away, "I don't need what you offer. I know who I am and what I am capable of achieving." And in such cases, I nod and agree that we would not be a good match for working together. Likewise, if this is something you are thinking right now, this may not be the book for you.

However, even if you think you know everything about yourself, consider the following questions:

- Have you reversed all the stuffing down and overshadowing influences of your past? If you haven't explored your past, then you can't fully know who you are in the present.

- Have you ever defined your Unique Personal Needs? When you do, you can immediately bring sanity and stability to any moment or decision.

- Have you ever determined which of your strengths are pseudo-strengths and which are superpowers? How about your weaknesses? Once these are known, there will be no doubt which levers to pull in order to catapult your success with power, ease, and elegance.

- Do you know how to measure the short and long-term success of your soul? Metrics defined by things that actually matter to you instead of sizing yourself in comparison to what others think?

These are all things you will have at your disposal by the end of this book, assuming you are willing to do the work. I won't lie, I am here to challenge you in ways you have never experienced before. My process requires an open mind and a soft heart. It requires a willingness to dig in to deep parts of your conscious and subconscious mind. It requires a tamed ego so you can uncover things about yourself you have yet to consider. That said, this revelation will happen easily and naturally if you simply follow the tried-and-true process that I have used with hundreds of clients before writing this book.

One of my favorite testimonials from a client sums up the transformation you are about to achieve perfectly:

> *"I now know how to live my life and earn a living by doing what inspires the best in me."*

This sort of feedback feeds *my* sense of self and tells me that my work is absolutely full of purpose. I am here to enliven and enlarge your vision of who you are and what you can achieve with that capacity. I am here to help you mine your own Soul Salt.

So, if you are ready to answer the deeper calling to that "something" inside that needs to be free ... If you are ready to live the rest of your life with the confidence, purpose, and fulfillment that you want, but can't seem to achieve ... If you want to live the rest of your life in a way that, on your deathbed you can say, "I'm so glad I lived a life true to myself!"

Congratulations, you are in the right place!

And, here's the great news—

By the end of this book, you will not only be aware of the "something" that wants to be set free, but you will know exactly how to identify your own personal Soul Salt and use these elements as a map to navigate life decisions and ensure you stay in alignment with your highest self.

If you are ready to dig up the salt of your soul, let's dive in!

If your eyes are opened, you'll see the things worth seeing.

—Rumi

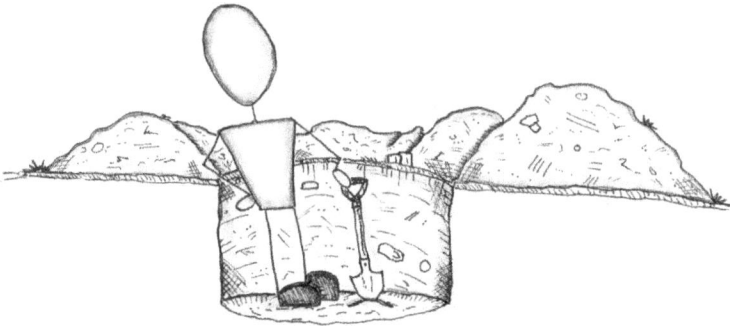

CHAPTER 1

Feeling *Less-Than* When You Are Actually *Greater-Than*

How often do you have self-doubt or low confidence? How about feeling stuck, or lost?

Do you want to be seen and valued by others, but know deep down that you don't fully value yourself? Instead, you stare in the mirror wishing your best aspects would magically "show up" and shine the way you know they can.

If you can relate, you're not alone.

More and more people are coming to the realization that they want something more out of life and out of themselves, but don't know how to coax it to the surface. This is exactly why the life-coaching industry is projected to be a $2.85 billion global industry by the end of 2022[1]. This is a pretty incredible number considering "life coaching" didn't really become a thing until the 1980s.

A BRIEF HISTORY OF PERSONAL COACHING

Thomas Leonard is widely thought of as the founder of life coaching as it's known today. He was a financial planner who took notice of how many of his clients needed guidance beyond achieving their financial goals. He noted that many sought help to better organize their lives, reach personal goals, and increase their overall happiness. Leonard gradually shifted his practice from financial planning to life planning based on these observations.

Throughout the rest of the 1980s, Leonard fine-tuned his methodology and began training other people as coaches. He founded Coach University in 1992 as the first official training organization, which is still active today. Leonard was also instrumental in founding the International Coaching Federation (ICF), which is responsible for publishing industry standards and ethics for coaches. It also provides credentialing for coaches and grants accreditation to coaching schools. The ICF is the benchmark for coaching excellence, thanks in large part to Thomas Leonard.

The coaching industry continued to grow at a relatively consistent pace for nearly two decades, then really took off around 2010. From 2015 to 2019 the number of credentialed coaches increased by 33%, totaling 71,000 worldwide.[2] Demand for life coaches is projected to grow by 19%, year over year, for the next several years.[3]

WHAT IS A LIFE COACH?

Some of you may already be well-versed in what a life coach is and does. For those of you who aren't totally sure, let me explain the role a bit:

You see, far too few of us were nurtured into awareness of who we really are and what we can do with all of our hidden skills, talents, gifts, and strengths. In fact, most people never take the time to figure out what all of those assets are. Instead, we've been told a story about who other people think we should be, based on beliefs they also didn't choose. So, they graciously hand down the same programs to us because … that's just how it's done.

This causes humans to sleepwalk through life. They go through the motions to get through each day just to do it all again tomorrow. Until, one glorious day, something inside wakes up just enough to bring realization that we want more. We figure out we aren't as happy as we could be—or at all in some cases. We might want more out of our career, partnership, or life in general, but not know how to get to the next level. This is where a life coach can help.

A qualified coach seeks to draw out "the essentials from the messy immediacy of the situation and to question premises and motivations in order to create clarity and understanding."[4] Or simply put, a coach helps you figure out where you're stuck, how to break through the barriers holding you back, and how to achieve goals you haven't been able to reach on your own. The goal is to help you become the best you possible in the shortest amount of time.

Here are a few statistics about the benefits of using a life coach:

- 80% of coaching clients say that they improved their self-esteem or confidence thanks to coaching.[5]

- One-on-one coaching has been shown to improve a client's psychological well-being and mitigate threats to mental health in the form of excessive and prolonged stress, low resilience, and poor satisfaction with life.[6]

- 68% of individuals who hired coaches were able to make back their investment, with the average return being 3.44x the cost of their coaching.[7]

- 73% of coaching clients say that coaching helps them improve their relationships, communication skills (72%), interpersonal skills (71%), work performance (70%), work/life balance (67%), and wellness (63%).[8]

- Coaching can help clients improve their self-awareness, confidence, leadership style, and their relationship to power, conflict, and personal life.[9]

As you can see, a good coach can improve a person's life in many areas. But it's up to each individual to realize they want more from life and to seek guidance on how to achieve it. The great news is, you're here! You bought this book and you're reading it, so you are one of the few who want to shortcut their journey to a better life. Congratulations on such a wise decision!

A coach helps you figure out where you're stuck, how to break through the barriers holding you back, and how to achieve goals you haven't been able to reach on your own.

I WANT TO BE YOUR COACH ... THROUGH THIS BOOK

I wrote this book because I know not everyone can access or afford a personal life coach. However, everyone deserves to become the most formidable, expansive, confident, and courageous version of themselves. I want this for you, and I have spent years training to be the one you want on your sideline.

I confidently step before you as a Master Certified Coach (MCC), earning my credentials through the largest coaching organization in the world, the International Coaching Federation (ICF). Only 4% of credentialed coaches have currently reached this master level. In fact, as of March 2021, there were only 1,327 of us in the entire world!

Since my initial certification as an MCC, I have continued to challenge myself to keep evolving in my craft:

- I was personally trained and mentored by Dr. Marshall Goldsmith, who many refer to as the top-rated executive coach in the world.[10]

- I am certified in Multiple Brain Integration Techniques (mBIT), a neuroscience method to find your way to better decisions and to understand why people make certain choices.[11]

- I am certified in *Conversational Intelligence®* and was personally mentored by its founder, the late Judith E. Glaser.

- Most recently I completed an *Accelerated Coach Excellence* course taught in part by Google's former head coach, Dr. David Peterson.

I continue to improve myself and my skills so I can be the most effective coach possible for my clients. What you will receive through this book is the culmination of years of experience, education, and training, not a watered-down version of what my clients get when they hire me for coaching. You are going to get the exact same process, guidance, and exercises you would receive if you worked with me one-on-one. This is a powerful program and can substantially change your life for the better, as long as you put in the work.

I'm going to pose questions that clarify what you believe about yourself. I will prompt you, and sometimes provoke you, to formulate a new understanding of who you are and what you can do with the discoveries you uncover.

We'll dig into your consciousness (and sometimes your subconsciousness) to find those wondrous and powerful parts that you know exist—but have been hidden for too long—and we'll let them shine.

We'll revise your concept of "self" in small steps and empower you to put some order to your findings. Then, I'll show you how to use the knowledge you uncover to create a guide to navigate future decisions with power and confidence.

So, if you'll have me, I'll be your coach, and you'll be the brave soul setting out to create your personalized system for navigating the world with confidence, strength, wisdom, and peace of mind. I cannot give you answers to the questions you are about to face. You really don't want me (or anyone else for that matter) telling you who you are and what to do with your life. Instead, we will partner in a "thought-provoking and creative process that inspires you to maximize your personal and professional potential, while unlocking previously untapped sources of imagination, productivity, and leadership," as explained by the ICF.

This is a powerful program and can substantially change your life for the better, as long as you put in the work.

BECOMING A CHALLENGE-READY ADULT

How many people are trapped in their everyday habits: part numb, part frightened, part indifferent? To have a better life, we must keep choosing how we're living.

—Albert Einstein

I've been coaching since 1998 and over the years my observations have aligned with the Einstein quote above. I'd wager that the biggest obstacle between you and the greatest version of yourself is that somewhere along the way *you stopped choosing*. Sure, maybe you kept learning and experiencing and putting new things in your head, but that's not good enough, is it?

It takes more than learning and gaining knowledge to become a confident, ever-evolving, problem-solving, challenge-ready adult. In fact, I propose it takes three significant steps:

Step One: We must wake up to the truth about who we are and what we can achieve. Not to put too fine of a point on it, our concept of self is primary.

The bulk of my coaching will support you to clear your mind of everything you thought you knew about yourself. Even some of your most cherished ideas will be challenged. In this new mental and emotional space, you'll be reeducated, develop your own strategic muscles, and stop depending so heavily on other people's theories and ideals for guidance. You'll be asked to make life-altering choices, which can be hard but very rewarding. Making a choice to be reeducated as an adult is massively courageous, but will allow you to sidestep the traps highlighted by Einstein.

Step Two: We need to take control of situations in our life by deliberately pouring the "source of our abilities" into a personal navigational system. Unless we keep this significant information front and center and continually updated, we tend to forget about it. We start to wander off track because, as you know, it is so, so easy to get caught up in life.

This book takes you through the same process I use with my coaching clients. You will complete several exercises throughout the book and log your discoveries as you go. Then, you will transfer them all to your personal map at the end. You will build on the guide throughout the book so that when you are finished, you will have your own navigation system, customized with your own Soul Salt elements. You will reference it often, just as you would on any other journey. This map can, and should be updated on a fairly regular basis in order to provide the best guidance for your current stage of life.

> *"We go through life willy-nilly ... trying to get things done. We forget we have strengths. We forget we have tools ... a lot of the time we're not living purposefully."*

> –Margie, recent client

Step Three: We need to acquire a personal, deliberate practice of using this map as we drive our lives forward. Just because you have a navigation system in your car doesn't guarantee that you won't take a wrong turn, or possibly even get lost. Developing a personal practice of deliberately navigating through life yields consistency. And consistency yields both success and satisfaction.

Again, chances are high that you've never had anyone coach you into creating this sort of deliberate practice. Your time for creating one has come. That's right, I've got you. We'll get to this step toward the end of the book and the best part is, you'll craft a practice that fits your life. You won't be forced to follow a contrived formula that assumes a one-size-fits-all posture.

We need to take control of situations in our life by deliberately pouring the "source of our abilities" into a personal navigational system.

BUT LYN, I'VE TRIED OTHER SOLUTIONS

While writing this book, I researched a stack of comparable titles. There are many great options out there from talented writers that focus on specific areas of your life. You may know some of them.

And yet, for as many books as I've consumed over the years (my home contains no less than four different libraries), I didn't find one that went as deep into self-actualization as I needed for my clients. None of these books coach you through a complete process. So, I wrote one that does.

You'd probably agree that there are many experts to help you become more productive. Numerous different authors show you how they successfully accomplished A, B, or C. There are endless options to help you learn how to do X, Y, or Z to improve your life. However, it's nearly impossible to find books designed to be by your side as you dig deep and discover things about yourself you've never known.

There are even fewer support systems that hold you accountable to use that information in an effective, individualized manner like this book does. So, if other programs haven't worked for you, this one will likely be the game changer.

One of the reasons I can say this with a certain degree of confidence is that many of my past clients have gained useful insight from outside sources. They came to me with pieces of the puzzle, but not the entire picture, which is what I am able to help people see.

The *StandOut* and *StrengthsFinder* are good examples of assessments that help you determine what you're good at. You can learn all about your personality by taking the *Myers-Briggs*, or the *Enneagram* tests. You may have learned about your communication style from a *DiSC* assessment. All of these are very useful tools, but typically provide only a piece of the puzzle.

We can capitalize on the usefulness of these pieces if you have your old reports laying around. They are a great asset, so I will reference them from time to time for those that have them. That said, if you haven't completed any of the assessments listed above, don't worry. You will get everything you need from the exercises I provide.

> You have numerous facets to the diamond that you are and you can use them all to ignite and empower your life.

I will show you that you are multi-dimensional. You have numerous facets to the diamond that you are and you can use them all to ignite and empower your life. You could do many things with all that great potential and skill, but you first have to know they exist! Let me guide you in discovering the many possibilities you possess in one, coherent process so you can stop going through life with just a few, if any, pieces of the puzzle.

SPEED BUMPS AND DETOURS

Every individual who comes into my practice brings a unique set of reasons why they haven't taken the steps I'm asking you to take. There are many common threads among them for why they aren't living their greatest life. The most common, by far, is that they are constantly reacting to life instead of intentionally creating the life they want. We must craft a map to help us navigate to a great life instead of wandering around in the dark and hoping to stumble upon it.

This makes sense, right? Without a guide, how can you fully understand where you are developmentally as an adult? And, if you don't know where you are, how can you figure out where you want to be? After all, we can't be fully responsible for something until we are fully aware of that something.

Former Harvard psychologist, Dr. Robert Kegan, has devoted much time and effort to his Development Theory. According to Kegan's theory, about 65% of the general population never become high-functioning adults. That means most adults haven't developed a full sense of self. Consequently, major traits that lend themselves to deepening personal wisdom also never develop, causing a lack of social maturity. We get caught looping around the factors that life throws at us instead of increasing our awareness of how to manage them better. This includes relationships with ourself and others.

When we take time to develop the traits that lead to personal wisdom, we can deliberately choose how we live. In Kegan's words, this is considered *self-authorship*. The bottom line is that you can either let life happen to you, or take control of it right this minute.

And if you're a tiny bit afraid to do what this book will require of you, I get it. That is totally normal and expected. I've seen the pattern repeat itself when the prospects of change and living a greater life arrive on one's doorstep—both excitement and fear are present. This pattern often indicates that you're on a path that is true for you.

When we take time to develop the traits that lead to personal wisdom, we can deliberately choose how we live.

Taking a risk, stepping into the unknown, and completing the exercises in this book will take you out of your comfort zone. When we take a risk in life, even if that risk can catapult you toward success and drastically increase your chances of achieving your dreams, the Autonomic Nervous System (ANS) causes fear to pop up. That fear is trying to keep you safe and often arises when someone points to a means that can make your life better than you've ever imagined.

Yes, taking a leap of faith by reading this book and applying its concepts means things are going to work out for the better. But first, let's confront that fear right now.

What are your fears? Write down anything that could keep you from enjoying the benefits of this book. Some examples may be:

- I am afraid I'm going to fail.
- I am afraid I'm not good enough to succeed.
- I am afraid I don't have what it takes to complete the work required in this book.
- I am afraid to get started on something new.
- I am afraid that if I grow, I'll leave people behind that I don't want to leave behind.
- I am afraid of changing and shifting parts of my life.
- I am afraid others will judge me.

Go ahead and write your specific fears down.

_____

_____

_____

Now determine the level of impact each fear will have on your results when it shows up.

- Rank each one that is a high impact with a score of 5.
- Each one that has a medium impact gets a 3.
- Each one that has low impact receives a 1.

If it's between these levels, you can assign a 2 or 4. Don't think about "if" it will raise its ugly head, just assume it will.

For each fear, rate the probability that it will trip you up or detour you away from success. If the probability is high, assign it a 5; Medium, give it a 3; and, if the probability is low, give it a 1.

Now, multiply the impact for each item by the probability and take notice of the score each fear receives.

Example: You are afraid to leave your comfort zone.

Impact – 3 (medium)

Probability – 3 (medium)

When you multiply 3 x 3 you get a Fear Score of 9.

Next, place the Fear Score on a number line like the one below. The lowest possible score for each fear is 1 with the highest possible score being 25.

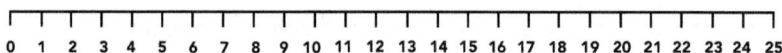

0 1 2 3 4 5 6 7 8 9 10 11 12 13 14 15 16 17 18 19 20 21 22 23 24 25

If your fears are somewhere close to the middle, or to the left of middle (which is usually the case), you can see you have less to fear than you imagined. Seeing a fear visually like this can help put it into proper perspective. Unless your Fear Score ranks a 25, you can easily work through the fear and transform it into empowerment.

Just like with your fears, who you are is going to become more visual, more out in the open, more tangible, and thereby more accessible to you.

Maybe you've tried mindfully and deliberately to develop as an adult. Maybe fear hasn't played that big of a role. However, there is a chance you got detoured from your development by the need to earn a degree or certification. Perhaps your need to work to provide for your needs was more important, or purchasing a home and raising a family took the front seat. We all have a story of how we became so caught up in the day-to-day that we didn't stop to make the huge decision to figure ourselves out. Just to drive this point home, here are some research-based reasons people don't reach their potential, even if they want to:[12]

- You don't know yourself. You were not allowed to feel your feelings and think your thoughts. You had to hide.

- You are living out someone else's values.

- You are driven by negative core beliefs. Remember 95% of these are hardwired by age 7, and we had zero input as to what we absorbed.

- We get stuck comparing ourselves to others.

- We're addicted to feeling bad and "less than."

- We try to control more than is possible to control.

Maybe you're not where you want to be yet, but that's okay. Data support that detours are a "thing" for sure. Hell, it wasn't like we were born with an owner's manual attached to our ankle. The good news is, we can use the work you do in this book to provide you with such a guide. Also, consider that detours are not full stops, they are just delays. You can still get where you want to go, it just might take a little longer.

Detours are not full stops, they are just delays. You can still get where you want to go, it just might take a little longer.

There is one common mistake I must warn you about when doing this kind of self-work: please don't delude yourself in thinking the path from A to B is a straight line. Too often, we think a journey will look like this:

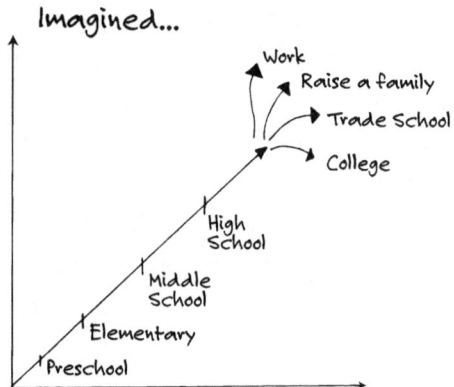

Imagined...

Work
Raise a family
Trade School
College
High School
Middle School
Elementary
Preschool

We've been led to believe that life is a straight path, when it is actually speckled with decision points. And all decision points either move us toward our goal, or become detours.

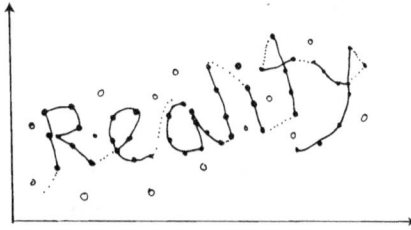

One example of this is choosing a career path. Did you know that an average American has twelve jobs throughout their life with an average tenure of 4.1 years with any single employer?[13] That sure does break the myth that you should go from pre-K to 12th grade, then into a job that you stay in forever, doesn't it? It also supports how much you need to be in the driver's seat of life, following your guide, with intention.

A LOT TO LOOK FORWARD TO

I assumed I was lost. Many of us do. I was busy doing work and service for organizations, businesses, and my church. I was beginning to question the beliefs I'd been taught as a kid. I felt a need to change and expand. I felt there was more to me and for me. That's why I hired you.

— Recently Graduated Client

You and your hopes, dreams, and personal power are what all this effort is about. The effort will positively alter the trajectory of your life. Every minute you spend on the upcoming exercises will bring you benefits for weeks, months, and years ahead. You will see, feel, and experience yourself differently. You will be more sure, true, strong, and focused.

Can you imagine approaching major life decisions with confidence and power? Can you imagine living a life that you craft instead of one you react to? Imagine how amazing it will be to come upon a detour and know exactly how to navigate the change without it disrupting your overall plan for life. It's going to be such a better, more fulfilling, and joyful experience! Now it's time to look forward and get going.

I've written this book as a substitute for us coaching together in person. So, roll up your sleeves and let's jump into the first exercise in the process. Your new "greater than" life begins in the next chapter!

Knowledge of self is the source of our abilities.

—Lao Tzu

CHAPTER 2

When Things Get Weird, Who Do You Call?

If there's something strange in your neighborhood, who you gonna call?

When there's something weird and it don't look good, who you gonna call?

An invisible thing's sleeping in your bed, who you gonna call?

If you're all alone and you wanna pick up the phone, who you gonna call?

—*Ghostbusters* Theme, adapted from Ray Parker Jr.

Fortunately, most of us don't battle ghosts for a living. We do find ourselves in pinches, tight spots, or stuck between a rock and hard place from time to time. Bouts of crisis or chaos are simply part of life. When you find yourself here, who do you call? Some of your calls come to me with concerns that sound like:

If you don't have a coach or someone close who can provide wise counsel, what do you do when you're facing difficulty and discomfort? How do you escape the grip of a pointless habit, or deal with feeling numb, fearful, or indifferent about your future? It's hard, if not damn near impossible, to choose and keep choosing a *greater than* life without someone to support—or tools to utilize.

As I mentioned in the last chapter, it would have been wonderful if your parents found your owner's manual fastened to an ankle at birth. When things get tough, you could flip to a page and find exactly what to do for yourself. But that didn't happen.

Or did it?

I believe you did come into the world with a guidance system. You have no doubt stumbled upon a certain number of its components as you've gained more experience in life—whether you are aware of them or not. The components of your guidance system are what I refer to as the *salt of your soul*. I contend that once I help you shine a light on these aspects of your personal identity, you will be equipped with the power to confidently make decisions and stay true to yourself. Even if you already have some awareness of these components, it will benefit you greatly to create a system to consistently use them when life gets weird. In fact, I'll make you a promise: you will never consider calling on the Ghostbusters once the *salt of your soul* is revealed. You'll have your own guide to reference and be able to easily navigate to the best decisions for a greater life. Plus, when populated with the greatest parts of you, this map also increases your satisfaction, confidence, and peace of mind. It's like knowing the secret sauce to the life you want.

You did come into the world with a guidance system.

The exercises in this book have all been user-tested by my clients and proven effective throughout my thirty-two years as a coach. However, I will reference plenty of studies and research, even scientific breakthroughs, to support our efforts as well. I'll be your guide; all you need is to be willing to commit to improving your life by completing all of the exercises.

DECISIONS AND INFLECTION POINTS

Let's start by considering three questions:

- When have you taken a stand?
- When have you opened your heart to new and exciting possibilities?
- When have you nurtured a dream?

Just think on these for now while I share some stories with you.

I remember the day when life as I knew it ended. I had three children running around, a house to clean, groceries to buy, laundry to do, a list of errands to run, and my spouse announced, "It is your job today to take care of me." Those ten words felt heavy with one too many unreasonable requests.

After years of stress and strain, something in me was finished. Things clicked into place like tumblers in an old safe's lock—emotions, thoughts, and beliefs converged with an undeniable flash of awareness. In a millisecond, without knowing how I knew, I recognized the line had been crossed for the very last time. I took a stand and made the tough and consequential choice to leave my husband and never return.

Then, the night after I started dating again, I was talking with a close friend about a guy I was seeing. I pivoted to look at her and unintentionally found myself extremely close to her face. I was moved by the safety, comfort, and the warm sensation of coming home to myself by being nose-to-nose with her. At this proximity the romantically laced sparks and intense chemistry were surprising, yet serene. Everything in my body, and in hers, felt right as rain as we adjusted our noses, lined up our lips, and followed the gravitational pull to press them together. The resulting *BAM* in my entire body brought awareness to what passion truly felt like for the first time. I decided to follow this path of the heart into personal reinvention and permanently left the realm of conventional heterosexual relationships.

Never once in my youth, or early career, did I aspire to start a small business. However, while making a career transition away from academics and toward business I encountered a business coach. I sat in session with her once and was hooked on the notion of starting my own coaching practice. This desire simmered in the background as I advanced up the corporate ladder. The dream got hotter and expanded until it forced me to sit down, make a plan, and start a certification program. I launched my side hustle practice and forfeited free time and weekends for 18 months as I grew a strong client base.

Today my company, Soul Salt Inc., is almost twenty years old. I can firmly state that it has continually provided the means to live life and earn a living by doing what inspires me.

These three stories are examples from my personal life about when I took a stand, opened my heart to new possibilities, and nurtured a dream. Hopefully they helped spawn memories of your own and make it easier to answer the questions. Take a moment and record your answers below.

When have you taken a stand?

_____

When have you opened your heart to new and exciting possibilities?

_____

When have you nurtured a dream?

_____

WHAT'S GOING ON HERE?

As I explain the rest of the story for each of my examples, consider your own experiences and ask, "What was going on for me?"

On the day I decided to leave my marriage, I took a stand because the thoughts in my mind, the feelings in my heart, and my gut instinct lined up in perfect synchronicity. I knew I was done. I could feel a deep, undeniable urge to have freedom and to be courageous enough to make that choice—no matter how uncomfortable or inconvenient it was. I was guided by my core values.

Then, the night I kissed a female for the first time, something opened up in my heart, mind, and instincts. All three indicated that there just might be more to love and life than I had allowed myself to know. I was tuning into an entirely new set of personal possibilities.

Finally, in the third story, my mind's eye was opened to imagine a career that woke up a vital and exciting something inside. And if I admit it, it felt a bit frightening too. Before this moment, I didn't recognize that some part of me had been asking the question, "What do you want to do with the rest of your life?" However, I could tell in my gut that having a coaching practice was an answer to my future. My heart lit up and instinct moved into action. There was no question that this decision was a *hell yes*! You just *know* when something is a *hell yes*! even if the thing you *know* takes effort and time to bring to fruition. I was surprised and overjoyed to learn what can happen when you satisfy a need you never knew you had.

What's going on in all three stories? *I was listening to my heart, following my gut, and using my head.* Can you sense a similar pattern within your examples?

WE HAVE FUNCTIONAL BRAINS IN OUR HEART, GUT, AND HEAD

Science now tells us that we have functional brains in our hearts and guts as well as our head. A functional brain has been defined as "the ability to perform a given cognitive or physiological task."[1] We make critical decisions our entire lives, so it's very handy to be able to enlist the hints from one's heart and the instincts of one's gut in addition to the insights of one's brain. On some level you may have already utilized your other functional brains. Have you ever said something like:

- In my heart of hearts, I knew I had to take the opportunity to . . .
- My gut didn't feel right about things. I said no to . . .
- In my mind's eye I envision . . .

Marvin Oka and Grant Soosalu published their book, *mBraining: Using Your Multiple Brains to do Cool Stuff*, in 2012. Shortly after, I traveled to Australia to certify in their coach training program where they revealed the intersection of neuroscience and ancient wisdom. My clients and I have benefited from this training ever since. The following quote from *mBraining* details the purpose of using multiple brains perfectly.

"... the main purpose for working with your multiple brains is not so you can 'do more' in life, but instead the aim is to live your life from your highest authentic expression and to live with greater wisdom in all your decision and actions."

HEART

It turns out, I can ask you questions that intentionally activate the 40,000 neurons in the heart's nervous system that are just like the neurons in your brain.[2] When you hear your answers, you are truly listening to the wisdom of your heart. According to Oka and Soosalu's book, *mBraining*, the heart is "the seat of love and desires, goals, dreams and values. When you are connected to something, you feel it and value it in your heart."[3] When you feel a deep sense of personal, moral rightness versus a rule-based ethic, you're listening to your heart.

> When you feel a deep sense of personal, moral rightness versus a rule-based ethic, you're listening to your heart.

GUT

Should you and I have a discussion regarding deep identity or your motivations, self-preservation, what to act on, and what not to act upon, we'd activate and enlist the support of your enteric nervous system, better known as your gut. Your gut stretches from approximately the top of your throat down to your "back door" and contains between 100 and 500 million neurons.[4,5]

When you feel a strong urge to take action, move away from danger, or detect a threat, the wisdom of your gut is at play. To be sure, if you've expressed an act of courage, your gut was part of the brigade leading the charge.[6]

Can you guess what brain would raise its hand to answer these types of questions?

- What do you envision for yourself in the future?
- What are the pros and cons?
- As you think about this, what thoughts come to mind?

See what I did there? I gave you a huge clue. If you thought these questions were geared for your head brain, you were correct.

When you feel a strong urge to take action, move away from danger, or detect a threat, the wisdom of your gut is at play.

HEAD

Your brain contains 86 billion neurons[7], which allows it to *think* in a much different manner than your heart and gut. It is the brain you're most familiar interacting with and the one you use for logical thinking, cognitive functions, reasoning, and making sense of things.[8]

You and I use our brain to get insights—those downloads that seem to fly in one ear, drop off a shiny and exciting idea, and fly out the other ear. You know you've had a *flash of insight* when you quickly forget it if you don't immediately write the shiny and exciting idea down. We also engage our brain to make sense of the world strategically and intellectually, and to take executive control (when we choose to) over our lives.

With all this said, can you guess what I'm about to tell you?

The next time you're in a difficult situation and you need to make a good decision, you can call upon your multi-brain capacity to offer up direction. This is one of the keys to your ability to self-author your way through life and navigate with confidence.

WHY HAVEN'T I DONE THIS BEFORE?

Rarely do I run into someone who has completed work as thorough and detailed as what we're about to accomplish. More often I hear clients say, "Why haven't I done this kind of work before? This was so useful. This was the game changer!"

There are plenty of books and programs out there that tell you how to design a well-lived and joyful life. There are those which offer up deliberate choices that support you to live on purpose. Some purport to help you release self-doubt, build self-compassion, and embrace who you are. Even others claim to show you how to create a life that matters to you. All of these are terrific endeavors, and I salute their creators. But here's the deal—the process in this book does all of the things mentioned while refraining from telling you the answers. It helps you learn who you are. This work will release doubt and build confidence because you will reveal the wonders of who you are from all three brains, then document them in your own handwriting.

Navigating life with a map created from your personal Soul Salt will help you meet the decision points, challenges, and changes you face with ease, elegance, and absurdity. Plus, you will learn that you can't go wrong following the sort of integrity, purpose-filled, strength-based components that we'll discover together. Get ready to confidently do life on your terms for the first time.

This work will release doubt and build confidence because you will gather evidence of the wonders of who you are from all three brains, then document them in your own handwriting.

WHAT DOES IT LOOK LIKE TO REFERENCE A MAP?

Following your own inner wisdom and crafting a guide built just for you looks a little different for everyone. My client Will was extremely uncomfortable with his job. His environment was toxic, and he felt stuck and undervalued. Will got a degree in accounting and was very good at it, but felt like that didn't fit any longer. Despite working his way up the corporate ladder and becoming a gifted Regional Finance Manager, he desperately wanted a change.

I know many of you can relate, or this is your situation right now.

Will heard about career coaching from his stepmother but hesitated to call me because he felt that "only high-level executives hired coaches to make career moves." He made up a story about not being smart enough to merit a coaching engagement. He worried that if he addressed his discomfort, the only way forward would mean a drastic pay cut. Will was equally concerned that even if he did move to a different employer, the conditions there might turn out to be even worse. He tried to tell himself to keep his head down and power through it. Turns out, he got to a point where he couldn't keep on forcing himself to trudge off to work.

Will ended up scheduling a free discovery session where I inquired about the outcomes he wanted from coaching. He responded, "I want to restore balance in my work-life equation. I want coaching to help me be a better contributor to my family." As we dug into what this might mean, he talked of finding a role, or even a new career path, that would be motivating and fulfilling. Will wanted a job that could reengage him in a manner where he cared again. He was tired of having his paycheck be the single reward for giving his time and energy. So, he hired me, and we started working together.

We worked through the seven exercises you're about to go through, and Will crafted his personal guide. I was impressed by how Will listened to more than the thoughts in his head. He also paid attention to his feelings and gut instincts. This led him to quickly find a new job in a more positive culture—a bridge job—that didn't have the toxins of the old job. The new role suited Will's talents and experience.

Once he felt comfortable in his new role, it became clear that the new environment still didn't tick the employment boxes he desired. More importantly, the new job didn't honor the person reflected by his guide. However, it was during this short stint at the new employment that Will came upon a job opportunity with a company called Bring a Trailer. One of the passions Will highlighted was his love for restored cars. Bring a Trailer was looking to hire a writer to create descriptions for their Online auctions. Will was not only interested in both writing and restored and souped-up cars, he had talent in both areas. His map agreed and Will got the job.

The culture at Bring a Trailer seemed like a dream come true. The type of work, the content of the work, and the hours, all afforded Will the work-life balance he desired. Will's wife was a schoolteacher, and they had two young children, so with a few minor adjustments to the family budget, the finances worked out as well.

Will's story is not an anomaly. I see it duplicated over and over in my practice. His story confirms that when you listen to more than your fears, are willing to look beyond your current constraints, and align with an inner guidance system, you really can find a way to earn a living and live a life that inspires you. You can have "all of what you want" and it might surprise you how easily it appears when you're willing to listen to your own wisdom and take action.

WISDOM OF THE ANCIENT GREEKS

Should you visit the Temple of Apollo at Delphi you'll see the inscription above in the forecourt. The translation is "Know Thyself."[9] Shakespeare included a similar concept in Hamlet with the line from Polonius, "To thine own self be true." Humans have sought to follow both admonitions for years and years. Today, you're in possession of the means to be able to fulfill the promise of both.

When you listen to more than your fears, are willing to look beyond your current constraints, and align with an inner guidance system, you really can find a way to earn a living and live a life that inspires you.

Once you and I finish the exercises in chapters 3 through 10, you'll have the critical information about your own identity that your head, heart, and gut can provide. Then we'll take specific pieces of that information and incorporate them into your very own navigation system—a tool you can use to drive and direct your life with confidence. One that was built by you, for you, and fully vetted by you.

So, if you have ever wished to know, without a doubt, how to be true to yourself and have greater amounts of:

- personal integrity,
- a stronger sense of your unique capabilities,
- a better means to right your ship,
- guidance to get your shit together,

Then you're on point with where we're headed.

Turn the page. Your journey begins there.

CHAPTER 3

Making Your Invisible Plumb Line Visible

A lot of the conflict you have in your life exists simply because you're not living in alignment; you are not being true to yourself.

Steve Maraboli, *Unapologetically You*

EVERY HOUSE NEEDS A STURDY FOUNDATION

You can build a beautiful home, but eventually it will sink, sag, or slip without a solid base. The same is true about your relationships, careers, or life in general. Your core values are like the foundation of a house—they provide the basis for actions, decisions, and behaviors over a lifetime that align with your integrity. This chapter is where we begin to uncover the foundation of the life you want.

Behaviors Aligned with Values = Personal Integrity

Without this alignment, life falls apart and you lose a sense of both purpose and direction. You may appear to be successful even though you may not feel successful. In fact, you may feel wobbly or lost more often than you'd like. You realize sometimes you've been chasing empty accomplishments.

Your core values are like the foundation of a house—they provide the basis for actions, decisions, and behaviors over a lifetime that align with your integrity.

A WAY TO STOP STRUGGLING, FIND DIRECTION, AND RIGHT YOUR SHIP

How often do you struggle to find direction or make big decisions? Do you wonder how to act in certain day-to-day situations? When you know your values, all of that becomes easier. Instead of doubt, you gain crystalized clarity. Instead of worry, you grow confidence.

Take Holly Tuckett, for example. I met Holly when she was exploring career options. Holly was an educator who had transitioned to being a mail carrier. Then, she certified as a fitness trainer, and later evolved into a real estate coach. None of these could satisfy her inner creative.

A storyteller at heart, Holly was determined to transform her lifelong interest in documentary filmmaking into a meaningful career that would move hearts and open minds. We worked for a time to distinguish her superpowers from weaknesses, and captured her *possibilities* (a concept coming up in a future chapter). But, when we pinpointed her core values as connection, loyalty and quality, something lit up for Holly. As her map came together, so did a distinct message—*become that thing you've always been inside your soul.*

Holly was brave enough to dive into filmmaking headfirst and wise enough to hold on to those values. She believes quality documentary filmmaking is born through strong connection and loyalty to both a film's storyline and the people through which that story is told.

As a filmmaker and cinematographer, Holly now uses those values to tell award-winning stories which have brought her critical acclaim and a satisfying career. Her 2018 film, "Church & State" and 2021's, "Anchor Point" have earned best feature-length documentary, best director, and other honors at the Nice International Film Festival, Sydney Women's International Film Festival, Cinequest, and the Paris International Film Festival.

Holly's core values continue to guide her in life and in the way she runs her business, Flying Hat Productions.

MY FATHER'S PLUMB LINE

When I was small, I watched my carpenter father build out a bedroom for my sister and me in an unfinished basement. He methodically chalked the lines for the walls and studs with his level and plumb line. I was in awe and inspired enough to want to build my own structure.

I gathered wood scraps, discarded nails, and borrowed a saw and a hammer with great enthusiasm. Then I joined a group of boys in the neighborhood and built my own little clubhouse in a nearby pasture. To this day, you could go into that basement room and enjoy a nap away from the summer heat and sun. The integrity of the structure is impeccable. The clubhouse, however, slipped into a heap of rotting wood long ago.

Do you ever feel like something you've built, or the life you've created, has slipped out of place?

The boys and I were not carpenters. Our skills were lacking, but our greatest mistake was being ignorant to the concept of alignment. Like the needle of a compass, your core values can illuminate the best direction. Aligning with your core values leads toward a meaningful life—one filled with purpose and authentic engagement.

The process of discovering one's core values involves more than picking them off a list. They are not items on a menu. Nor are your values a one-and-done proposition. Life throws us curve balls and, as Einstein mused, *we forget to choose the life we want.* Unless we are in conversation with our values on a regular basis, things start to veer offtrack.

Aligning with your core values leads toward a meaningful life—one filled with purpose and authentic engagement.

Maybe you can relate to one of the top account executives at iHeartMedia, Kristen Henderson. She is often ranked in the top five performers in her group. She recently attended a SoulSalt, Inc. Bootcamp during which she created her own map.

Kristen was killing it with her national accounts (which are much bigger and harder to land), but her local numbers were struggling (which are much smaller budgets) and she was very unhappy. She had a really hard time with the fact that she wasn't performing at 100% across the board. However, by going back to her core values, Kristen realized she needed a paradigm shift in how she looked at her business and where she focused her energy. She realized she hadn't failed at all! Kristen rose to a level she had been trying to achieve for years but didn't realize she crossed the finish line. This made it much easier to be happy with her current success, reevaluate and set new goals, and stay in good alignment with her values.

Your values have been present and working behind the scenes for much of your life. You may think it's easy to sit down and churn out a complete list of core values without digging. However, for more than twenty years that I've been coaching, 98% of my clients have been surprised by their discoveries after completing the upcoming exercise. I'm guessing you will be too.

LET'S DIG!

Stop following the crowd. Avoid being part of a mindless herd. The following nine steps will guide you to the first draft of your very own core values. Don't forget to notice how your body responds while doing these steps as well. Invite your heart and gut to activate even more than your head, if possible. The coaching questions I provide for you in this exercise speak to all your brains.

Step One: Which three people (or characters) are you drawn to with respect or admiration? Think about who you'd enjoy being more like. Maybe you know these people. You may only know of them. These people may have passed on years ago, or they might be alive today.

Write the name of two or three people on the lines provided here.

_____

_____

_____

By each name, list out the words, phrases, descriptive traits that pull your attention and high regard to each person.

Step Two: Remember in chapter two when you were asked to recall a time when you took a stand? What came to mind? Think back to situations when you took a stand for something. Focus on what you were standing for. Be less interested in the story about taking a stand and see if you can identify the essence of your motivation.

Write your thoughts here.

_____

_____

_____

Step Three: Stop and consider yourself to be like a magnet. Magnets are made up of pure iron and a combination of other elements such as nickel and cobalt. If we took a magnet and pushed it along a stretch of sand, the magnet would appear to have grown a layer of fuzz. The fuzz is actually tiny shards of pure iron, or magnetite, attracted to the electrifying power of the magnet. In other words, like has attracted like.

In this scenario, you are analogous to being the magnet. Notice again the words and phrases you used to describe the people mentioned in Step 1. Review the words about your "take a stand" moment.

Consider each word to be analogous to the iron filings. Every word you've recorded has more to do with you than anything else. Each word is reflecting back to you a deeply personal, highly relevant part of your identity. What you wrote about others is a mirror back to you. These words reflect part of your core value system.

Let that sink in. How does it feel if you allow yourself to enjoy these pieces of yourself? It's quite possible you have never understood these aspects of yourself as well as you do now.

Step Four: Now, take a shot at listing out what a *Top Ten List of My Values* might include. Write your answers here.

_____

_____

_____

_____

Step Five: Go to the list of *Core Values* found in Appendix A at the back of this book. Place a number 1 by any entry that resonates, giving you a similar sensation as those we just spoke of in Steps One and Two.

For example, if the word *freedom* speaks to your heart with a strong ferocity, assign it a number 1. If a word has the opposite effect, label it with the number 3. If a word falls flat, or feels like it doesn't have a strong connection with you, assign it a 3 as well. If a word feels neutral or elicits little response from you, assign it as a 2.

Step Six: Compare the Top Ten List you generated in Step Four with all those you just designated with the number 1. Using both this list and all those words in the appendix that have a 1 by them, create a new list. We'll call this your *Top Dozen* (you can have a regular dozen or a baker's dozen).

_____

_____

_____

_____

Step Seven: Cut your list in half. That's right. Pick your top six words. Sometimes people like to configure words together that seem to have a similar theme to them. It is okay to narrow your list down to six themes if you'd like. Or you can go hardcore and just have six single words.

Step Eight: Now cut that list down to three. That's right, narrow your list of six down to three words, or three themes.

Write your three remaining words below and be sure to add descriptions and definitions so you refine what each one means to you. Don't worry, I won't ask you to narrow the list down any further!

_____

_____

_____

Take a look at what you've excavated. You now have the first draft of your very own core value system. Some folks call these their *North Star,* while others refer to them as the *Compass of Their Heart.* You're looking at elements of you—the salt of your soul—that are formidable. These are pieces of you that cannot be taken from you. Your values are indestructible, undeniable aspects of your Soul Salt.

These are your guiding principles and the foundational aspects of all your past success and the success still to come. As you look at your values, you may remember times in your life when they were active. As a personal example, I realized my values were active when I was fighting back with my grandmother.

A great way to solidify your values after completing the work in this chapter is to share what you discovered with a loved one or friend. Or, do some reflective writing and ask yourself, *"Where and when have my values guided me in the past?"* But, before you go any further, record your values at the end of this chapter and notice how it feels to start to populate the elements for your map. They will act like an anchor for the work to come. After you've written them down, let's put them into action and see what happens.

TEST DRIVE YOUR SYSTEM

If you don't understand your values, you may violate them without realizing it. You're positioned to have a greater understanding of two phrases I'm sure you've heard before:

1. Know thyself.
2. Be true to yourself.

Researchers confirm that when people have a clear set of values:[1,2]

- Making big life decisions is easier, as is pursuing passions, long-term career goals, and relationships.
- They are less likely to engage in destructive thought patterns, especially in difficult life situations.
- They tolerate physical pain more easily.
- They have greater self-discipline and focus when studying or working.
- They have more resilience.
- Their social connections are stronger.

You've just uncovered the most unshakable parts of your soul. Now, challenge yourself to align with your values and allow them to lead the way through a series of days. Try picking one of your core values to lead your actions, thoughts, and decisions. Align with this value as often as you can. Live in alignment with your values and feel the formidable nature of your own Soul Salt. Also, note when you don't align. What actions take you out of alignment and what brings you back in line with being true to yourself? Use a day-book or notebook to record your experiences. Or, download the free tracking sheet at www.soulsalt.com/book.

A great way to solidify your values after completing the work in this chapter is to share them with a loved one or friend.

PRO-TIPS TO CONSIDER

As you experiment with aligning and acquainting yourself with your values, consider these tips:

Stick with three values … for now. Did you resist when I pushed you to only pick three values? I have good reasons for this—too many leaves you scattered, confused, and feeling divided; and too few won't provide a stable enough base to rely on. Think of it like sitting on a two-legged stool. Ultimately, you want to be aligned to enough anchor points to be stable, but you don't what the chaos of chasing after too many masters.

Make sure the values you chose actually belong to you. Gut-check them. Assure that they have not been imposed on you by an external force. Some clients think if *God*, *church*, or *family* don't make it to the top three values, then something must be wrong. These words might represent something very important to you without being a core value, and that's okay. They may fit better into a future part of your guide that we've not yet addressed, so trust the process.

All of your values are equally important. If words like *adventure* or *beauty* are in your final three, don't question their importance. These, like so many words on the core value list, are not frivolous. Don't talk yourself out of the importance of your values. These two words are of the variety that get questioned the most. And yet, when you start aligning behaviors and decisions with your guiding principles, life has more integrity. The way you feel about life is honest, more real, and filled with more flow.

Don't stick a list of your values on the wall and forget about them. Continue through the book to the very end. Understand all the components you uncover. This way you can navigate your life with them in concert with the other elements of your greatness.

YOU ARE PRIMED

Now, you are prepared to take more authentic action and know with confidence how to *be true!* Just as you sifted, sorted, and contemplated to get to your final three values, so will you have to navigate life. There will be difficult decisions with tension between various parts of you. Your head will say one thing while your heart says another. Your gut will want to take action and your heart or head might disagree. You have completed some hard work.

You have created a new neurological connection to follow in the future by forcing yourself to give up certain values when choosing your final three. That tension is important to note. Now you know what it feels like to split hairs and align with the greater of two goods. These are hard decisions to make and you've shown yourself you can do it. Don't let yourself forget that achievement.

I invite you to keep those newly discovered values front and center while you continue to move through the rest of the chapters. There will be plenty more exercises where they will help you to align with your best self. Looking forward, we're going to pivot from values and explore what I refer to as *Unique Personal Needs.*

VALUES

List your 3 Core Values Below:

1. _____

2. _____

3. _____

CHAPTER 4

Are You a Raisin or A Grape?

Y ou can survive without oxygen for about four minutes before permanent brain damage occurs. More than six minutes and most of us would die.[1] Depending on our body's needs, age, and other factors, we can survive three to four days without water.[2] Take away our food and some of us will be able to exist for a couple of months.[3] These are basic facts about human *needs*. Hopefully, you haven't tested their limits.

There is another sort of need that I call a Unique Personal Need. I am 100% certain you have at least one, if not several that are starving, hungry, and gasping for air at this very moment. You may not be aware of this sort of need, but when it is left unaddressed it will flounder quietly in the background of your life. Somewhere, something is sucking away your capacity to be your best.

"IT'S JUST ONE OF THOSE DAYS?"

Consider the days when, despite eating, drinking plenty of water, and getting proper sleep, you feel like things are *off*. In fact, you feel more like a shriveling raisin than a plump, robust grape. What's going on when this happens? What's behind the difference? Let's examine what might be happening when you feel more like a raisin and less like a grape.

By definition, a *need* is an essential element. If we ignore it, we pay a price. If we meet our needs, we become vital, vibrant, and quite capable. Let's establish what I mean about feeling like a raisin versus a grape by sharing a tale of two bike rides:

Several years ago, I started mountain biking. Veteran riders warned me to "eat before you're hungry, drink before you're thirsty, and rest before you're tired. Especially when riding on backcountry trails." I always followed this guidance … until the one time I didn't. Somewhere in a four-hour ride my legs gave out—I mean they just stopped pedaling. A signal was moving from my brain down the chain, but my legs didn't pick up the cue. Forced to sit and rest for an hour, it eventually became possible to walk (not ride) back to my jeep. There I rested again and replenished with a small supply of electrolytes and liquid. This was a tough way to learn never to neglect my basic needs again.

A need is an essential element. If we ignore it, we pay a price.

Fast forward to the year I trained for an Xterra sprint triathlon. Nine months of disciplined training went into the effort. I brought along plenty of water, electrolytes, and appropriate gear and began to notice the supportive effects during the second, or biking leg of the race. I was surprised that even while pedaling, my legs recovered on the downhill slopes and semi-flat portions of the trail. After the final transition and into the running part of the event, I could tell how well I was conditioned. I had plenty of gas to finish strong. Although this was my first triathlon, effort and preparation paid off and landed me a 2nd-place medal in my division.

In one scenario, I ignored the needs of my body. In the other, I honored and met the needs. The outcomes were drastically different. But life isn't a bike ride. It is not a bike race either. (Although some people act like it is.) When feeling like a shriveled raisin, it is because a Unique Personal Need is not being met.

YOU HAVE UNIQUE PERSONAL NEEDS

We all experience a constant cycle of needing sleep, water, and food. It's part of being human and is a basic survival need. A Unique Personal Need (UPN) is a requirement specific to you. You *need* certain things in order to be at your best. Not want, need. These personal and unique things are not shared by another living human being. No one needs what you need exactly as you need it. Consequently, your one-of-a-kind needs merit your attention. There are consequences, although often not life-threatening, when you ignore them. Over time, not knowing or caring for your UPNs can be harmful, and sometimes even dire. Unique Personal Needs are must-haves for a life that is fulfilling.

Let's get specific. UPNs don't show up on diagrams such as Maslow's Hierarchy of Needs. In fact, it would be impossible to build an all-inclusive list. The variety of UPNs per human being is expansive, yet approachable. So, rest assured you have UPNs. You may already be familiar with some of them, but I bet there are many more you are unaware of at this moment. It's a surprise to every client when I help them uncover an unknown need. Once we're aware of them, we are responsible for establishing a pattern for meeting them.

You need certain things in order to be at your best. Not want, need.

WHAT WE ARE REALLY TALKING ABOUT

You have UPNs that are as distinct as your thumbprint. I'm sure you are eager to find out what a few of yours might be, but first, I want to prime you for the upcoming exercises by sharing some UPN examples from my client base.

Mary is a seasoned journalist and managing editor for one of the world's biggest news agencies. She sought my coaching expertise to help reinvent her career and we uncovered a UPN in the process. Mary shared the following in one of our sessions:

> *"Lyn, I have discovered one of my UPNs. I need to get up in the morning and brew my coffee. Then I take a shower, get dressed, and grab my coffee to go in the car. I love it, and I need this morning ritual, including the drive to work. I need to feel dressed for work, ready with my coffee, and in my car commuting to work to be at my best. I never realized this until I was working from home and had a comparison. When I have my morning ritual, I'm energized and alive."*

Then there was Wes, a former employee of Amazon and currently a designer at Google. Wes and I discovered their UPNs for time, preparation, and planning. If put on the spot in a meeting, Wes is hard-pressed to access the best ideas. They will freeze and feel uncomfortable in these situations. So, we crafted a three-step strategy to counter such moments. Now, Wes will thank the person for the question and repeat the question to buy a bit of time. Then, they deliver the idea their mind has crafted during that time.

As for me, it took some time to realize that I am a visual thinker who processes thoughts out loud. I often feel like life would be easier if I could open a window in my mind to let the ideas out. So, I installed a large glass "thinking board" in my office. I draw, sketch, write, and allow a brain dump to appear so that my team understands what I'm trying to communicate. Embracing this UPN has helped me be a stronger asset to the company, my clients, and the team.

HOW DO I IDENTIFY MY OWN UPNS?

There are many ways by which you can identify a UPN. Let me share three and allow you a chance to sample each one. Who knows what we'll find! Knowing your UPNs and then having a practice for getting them met does two big things for you: One, it increases the amount of sanity, stability, and sustainability you enjoy; and two, it stops those pesky unmet needs from running rampant through your behaviors. You know, the kind that drive you and those around you a bit crazy.

Let's discover what you need!

Exercise #1:

Go back through your answers from the work you did in Step Six of Chapter 3, your "Top Dozen" values. Notice words or phrases on that list that feel like they might be a UPN. For example, a client mentioned that there were, "… pieces of me on that list that didn't make it to the final three values. But somehow, they are extremely important to me. What do I do about that strong connection to these concepts?"

Some of the words on your *Top Dozen Values List* may feel the same way to you. No matter what you did or didn't do with these words, recognize that some of them may also be UPNs. Here's a way to distinguish that information for yourself.

It is probably part of your core value system if the word or concept feels like it is:

- a personal guiding principle;
- a component of giving direction and clarity to make decisions;
- a part of my inner compass;
- something that my heart consistently gravitates toward;
- a North Star that is a reference to stay on track;
- a word that I sense a high vibration with;

It is probably a UPN if the word or concept feels like it:

- quiets down a part of your life when it gets attention;
- is something you need a regular dose of to be at your best (like fuel or juice);
- is a stabilizing factor in your life;
- increases sanity when you meet its requests;
- helps you sustain yourself over a long period of time;
- provides a scratch for a particular itch;

Make a short list of the words or phrases that have come to mind so far. Again, remember that a word may represent a UPN and a value. It is rare to have all three values completely mimicked in your UPNs. Yet, you may see a relationship between them.

_____

_____

_____

Exercise #2:

Take yourself through the following flow chart of choices. As you go through the flow chart, keep in mind this critical question: *Am I more like _____ or _____.* Chances are you will relate to some of each option. Yet, as you flow through the questions, pick what you tend to be like the majority of the time.

Step One: I am more:

> **X** – Active, animated when I speak, quick and decisive, eat and walk faster than most;

Or,

> **Y** – Deliberate, softer and slower when I speak, eat and walk slower than most, more passive than most.

If you chose X, move to Step Two-X. If you chose Y, move to Step Two-Y:

Step Two-X: I am more like:

> **E** – Often referred to as direct, can come across as competitive, willing to take a few risks, often feel confident in my capacity;

Or,

> **F** – Enthusiastic, filled with optimism most of the time, greatly appreciates social recognition, ideas flow in an almost unending cascade.

Step Two-Y: I am more like:

> **G** – Analytical, appreciative of quality and accuracy, more deliberate than most, likes to plan;

Or,

H – Appreciative of stability, values cooperation, often told you are patient and loyal, like to approach things with diplomacy.

Which letter did you identify with the most? Here is a list of UPNs often associated with each letter:

E. You have a potential need for:

- **Getting results.** If you can't accomplish, or win, or get a result, you get frustrated.
- **Challenges.** If you don't face a few challenges along the way, you don't feel as fulfilled as you'd like.
- **Being in charge.** You don't shy away from taking the lead and being in control. In fact, you like to make decisions.
- **Action.** You thrive when things are happening.
- **Directness.** You feel most comfortable when direct and succinct language is used.
- **Identifying tasks.** You like to check things off your list or move things off your plate.
- **Speed.** You like to move and act with speed.
- **Efficiency.** You like things to be done efficiently.
- **Bullet Points.** You have a great appreciation for those who can deliver information in bullet points.

F. You have a potential need for:

- **Sharing your ideas and dreams.** It is satisfying when you can tell others about your desires and ideas.
- **Sharing your feelings.** You don't shy away from talking things out and discussing feelings.
- **Brainstorming.** You're full of ideas and generating lots of them can be a need for you.

- **Motivating others.** You need to inspire others in order to feel fulfilled.

- **Be noticed for your contributions.** If you don't get feedback on where you're succeeding, a part of your effort feels lackluster.

- **Connection with people.** You do your best with teams and relationship-oriented work.

- **Room to be nimble.** You can move quickly and being nimble helps you operate at peak performance.

- **Trying new things.** You need to have variety and try new things.

- **Honoring your gut instincts.** You have a great sense of intuition and using it can be defined as a need.

G. You have a potential need for:

- **Data, facts, information, etc.** You have a need for such things so you can do your deliberations.

- **Space.** You need time and space to think things through.

- **Moderate pacing.** You need things to move at a moderate pace so you can look at all the angles.

- **Procedures and processes.** You do your best work when procedures, rules, and processes are honored.

- **Looking at things in writing.** You do best when you can look at a document, or the details.

- **Respected for expertise.** You have the ability to do deep dives into situations or information. Thereby, it is deeply satisfying if you are respected for having an area of expertise.

- **Asking questions.** You need to be able to ask questions and get further information.

- **Getting down to business.** You often like getting down to business instead of spending time on frivolous things.

- **Contemplation time.** You do well when given time to make decisions or come up with ideas and solutions. Being asked your opinion on the spot doesn't always net your best work.

H. You have a potential need for:

- **Peace.** You do your best work when things flow in a harmonious manner.

- **Cooperation.** You need others to work together or with you in order to get things done.

- **Inclusion.** You need all voices at the table to be heard and understood.

- **Boundaries.** You are quite empathic and will pick up on the energy and needs of others. If you don't put up and keep boundaries, you feel drained and weakened.

- **Steadiness.** You excel when things are consistent and reliable.

- **Time and space.** You do your best work with patience and space to work things out over time.

- **Agreements and clarity.** You need agreements and clarity around expectations when in relationship with others.

- **Respect.** You need to be seen, heard, and valued even though you may be quieter and more passive than most. You may have learned that the squeaky wheel gets the attention. You need attention, but not for being squeaky.

- **Authenticity.** If things are not authentic, you are not interested. You have a need for a high degree of genuineness.

What resonates with you as being a UPN? Remember, the definition of a Unique Personal Need is something you must have, be, or do in order to perform at your best. When a UPN gets met it brings you a greater sense of stability and sanity.

Capture your first list of UPNs:

_____

_____

_____

Exercise 3:

What is universal and general can sometimes be personal. Sometimes it's helpful to reference a list of universal needs. We can find pieces of ourselves in a collective and shared set.

You will find a list of _needs_ offered up by the Center for Nonviolent Communication[4] on the book resources page of our website, www. soulsalt.com/book. It's not uncommon to find a word or two that speaks to your head, heart, and gut in regards to a UPN. Go ahead and take a peek. See if something sparks a connection. If so, write the word or words here:

_____

_____

_____

STEP BACK, TAKE A BREATH, NOW LET'S GET IT!

Well done!

By now you should have a stronger sense of what a UPN is, and have a list of some of your specific needs. As you look over your list you might notice a few UPNs in great need of your attention. Not all UPNs are created equal and not all require immediate attention. In fact, you may find that once you get a few UPNs met, other items on your list feel satisfied and fade away naturally.

It is now your job to start meeting one of your UPNs so you know what this might feel like.

Use the lines below to make a short, prioritized list of your UPNs.

_____

_____

_____

_____

_____

Next, pick one UPN off your list. If you have a sense of which one you'd like to focus on first, choose that one. If not, randomly pick one.

These questions will engage your head, heart, and gut (H/H/G) brains if you'd like their support to decide where to start:

- Which of your needs will you pick first?
- What do you feel would be a good place to start?
- Which one motivates you the most?
- What could you see happening first?

Once you've made your decision, sit for a short spell and brainstorm what you could do to address this UPN. Include a friend or family member if you'd like help generating ideas. Next, you will want to craft a plan of action and start experimenting with how you can appropriately satisfy this UPN.

For example, I focused on meeting a UPN back when my children were small. I noticed how much it bothered me to walk into a room where one of the bulbs in a light fixture was out, or missing. Like with a basic human need that was not getting met, it made me feel *less than* and *shrunken* when it occurred. I decided to experiment with how it might feel to have the right amount of light in each room. I made an inventory of all the sizes and wattage requirements of appliances and fixtures. I purchased a reasonable supply of bulbs and stored them in a plastic container. As I noticed a need for a new bulb, I quickly grabbed a ladder (if required) and the bulb in question. Within seconds my energy and my capacity to function improved. Who knew that having enough light in a room was something I needed to be a better version of myself. Until then, I had no clue.

I'd love to hear about your experience meeting the need of a UPN you had previously ignored. Post about it on social media and tag #soulsaltinc, or send us an email at info@soulsalt.com.

IN CASE YOU NEED A NUDGE

Sometimes clients find themselves resisting the concept of meeting their own UPNs. The conditioning to take care of other people's needs first has left them feeling a bit stuck. Many of us were told that we must take care of others, sometimes to the detriment of our own progress. Dr. Ross Rosenburg calls this condition Self Love Deficit Disorder (SLDD). Do you feel more concerned with caring for others than taking care of your own life? Here's a reason to consider a change:

Experience shows that the better you are at addressing your own UPNs, the better you are at giving healthy support to others. And, as an additional bonus, when you take care of your own UPNs you are better able to put healthy boundaries into play, further protecting your energy. Plus, if you wear yourself out to take care of others first, what happens to them when you're so worn down that you can't give anymore? Do they just wither away because you're not there to save the day? Do they turn into raisins? Meeting your UPNs and taking them seriously allows you to serve at a greater level, so please don't neglect them.

The better you are at addressing your own UPNs, the better you are at giving support to others.

Let me mention one last thought on this topic of taking your UPNs seriously. You may occasionally feel like your UPNs are frivolous and unimportant. One question I would ask in this situation is, "What happens if you're so busy living that you don't make time to go to the restroom?" Things get clogged up and nasty pretty darn quickly. In comparison, challenge yourself to meet one UPN so your life-flow doesn't get backed up. If you feel the spark of life, the enlivened, enlarged sense of who you are, then hold onto that thought. A lifetime of meeting UPNs is a simple way to exponentially improve the quality of your life.

As you create a practice of meeting UPNs, consider yourself to be an "athlete" of life. The best sports athletes have many people relying on them to take good care of themselves. That way, when it's "go time," they can step up and play the part the team needs them to play. There's a lot of individual self-care that goes into making a powerful team player.

You have one life to live. It is up to you to meet your needs like an adult. It is up to you to bring the sanity, stabilizing factors, and sustaining support that you get from meeting a UPN. Again, when we give consistent support to self, we are better fit to serve others. And this helps make the world a better place for everyone.

WATCH OUT FOR ROOKIE MISTAKES

Let's discuss a few tips that can help you avoid some rookie mistakes.

- Don't reference a single source as "The Source" for finding all of your UPNs because you're more complex than that. Simply keep an eye out for new UPNs to crop up. It is possible to go a full lifetime without identifying all your possible UPNs. Addressing some of the obvious ones is far better than addressing none.

- Life is a long series of getting needs met. Don't let yourself go too long between seasons of working on your UPNs. It is okay to occasionally rest. Just don't forget they are a thing and need your focus.

- Don't ignore your UPNs and definitely don't try to negotiate them away. Do so at your own peril. When a plane is too busy flying to land for fuel, bad things happen.

- Avoid being critical or judgmental of your UPNs. This is a sure-fire way to undercut the power and excellence that is waiting for you. When we meet needs, we fuel ourselves with the juice of life.

You have one life to live.
It's up to you to meet your needs like an adult.

ABOUT THAT RAISIN OR GRAPE QUESTION

By now, you are either engaged and experimenting with meeting a UPN, or you are about to. Enjoy the process and have some fun. I noticed how much joy came into my client Sierra's life when she started validating her UPNs. She's an energetic, bright entrepreneur who thrives when she receives positive acknowledgement. She set up a system for capturing client feedback and this lifted her energy and enthusiasm. It was like she finally had jet fuel (or grape juice) in her pack. The fun and excitement that grew were motivating and delightful.

I will always light up when I recall what happened for my client Andrew when he started to honor his need to write. Andrew has the soul of a writer and is a published author. Once he set aside time to write, so much shifted for the better. His home and personal life, as well as his professional path, are more authentic and peaceful.

Like Andrew, Sierra, and every other client I've had the pleasure of knowing, you have UPNs too. Now, you should have the tools to discover what they are. When you find them, feed them. Tackle them in a systematic fashion (think about my light bulb process). Notice how much saner you feel when you do. Note how much more stable life seems and how much easier it is to sustain the good parts of life for longer amounts of time.

UPNs are a part of your life leadership requirements for the kind of life that expands and ignites the best in you. This is a good time to publish one or two of your UPNs on at the back of this chapter. They will eventually be plotted on your map to keep in front of you until they no longer require your attention.

Keep the adventure alive and enjoy the work you just completed. Notice how it feels to live in alignment with your core values. Take note of the difference it makes when you acknowledge a UPN and get it met. Later in the book we'll address how to use the guide in its entirety, but first, the next exercise helps you pinpoint the mighty muscles of your very own superpowers! Hang onto your hat because you'll be flying high and fast once you plug into these parts of yourself.

 **NEEDS**

List up to 5 Unique Personal Needs Below:

1. _____

2. _____

3. _____

4. _____

5. _____

CHAPTER 5

Superheroes or Villains—Who Rules Your Universe?

How well can you match these superheroes with their superpowers?

1. Wonder Woman, 2. Captain America, 3. Black Panther, 4. Wolverine, 5. Black Widow

A) Skilled martial artist and acrobat. Extreme abilities to hunt and engage in combat.

B) Immortal, super strong, magical genius with an invisible flying craft.

C) Muscles and bones capable of breaking wood and steel with a single blow. A destruction-resistant shield.

D) Multilingual champion in Taekwondo, Kung Fu, Sambo and more. Also dubbed one of the "most dangerous operatives."

E) Possesses retractable adamantium-plated bone claws. Regenerates with help from an indestructible skeleton.

1-B, 2-C, 3-A, 4-E, 5-D

Y ou may have dreamed of being faster than a speeding bullet, or imagined the experience of lifting a teetering bus of children from the edge of a cliff. How would it feel to have superpowers? I'm asking because you should know—you have them. But chances are you know the answers to this quiz better than you know your own superpowers.

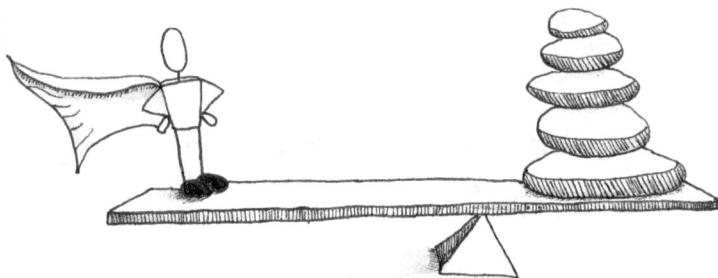

YES, YOU HAVE SUPERPOWERS

At any given moment, you are using a superpower. You effortlessly use them to do outstanding things. In fact, it feels terrific when you enlist your superpowers and they always get extraordinary results. You make the world a better place when you use them.

Shannon Dee followed me from our days working at Franklin Covey Coaching. She supports the administrative and operational functions at SoulSalt, Inc., and manages the never-ending scheduling of clients. She fits critical meetings into my calendar. She has created a method for balancing client needs with profitability requirements. Her precise placement of coaching sessions into each week has improved our profitability. This sort of organizational superpower is something I'm grateful for her every single day.

You have potent superpowers like Shannon. Think about things you are good at *and* love doing. Things you not only enjoy, but can improve and grow over time. Superpowers are things that take little effort, and when you do them, you make them look easy.

Be sure to note that all these elements must be present to qualify a strength as a superpower:

- You are good at it.
- You love doing it.
- You can improve and grow it.
- You don't need to exert much effort to perform it.
- You can easily do big things with it.

Voices at Gallup®, Marcus Buckingham, and others have been preaching to us for decades to know our strengths (a.k.a. superpowers). You may have taken their useful assessments in the past. If you're like most, your results are sitting in a file folder on your desktop or in a drawer somewhere.

Superpowers—things you are good at, love doing, take little effort, and when you do them, you make them look easy to the onlooker.

Being aware of your superpowers *and* using them is the point. If you're not deliberate about keeping them front and center, they fade. Think how vulnerable superheroes are without their superpowers. The same is true for you. Take a moment and jot down what you think your superpowers are.

Did you come up with a few? Are you sure they are all superpowers, or could some of them be pseudo-strengths? Let's find out.

THE ILLUSION OF A PSEUDO-STRENGTH

Two activities that suck attention away from utilizing our superpowers are spending too much time and energy using pseudo-strengths and fixing weaknesses. Let's address pseudo-strengths first because you definitely have them, but chances are high you're unaware of what they are.

Pseudo-strengths look like superpowers to those who witness you using them. You can accomplish above average work when you use them and may even receive specific, or extra assignments because you can make short work of tasks requiring their use. Others are impressed with your ability to use your pseudo-strengths, which may feel good if you are being recognized, but you definitely don't want their opinions to drive your career progression or success path. The best way to make sure that doesn't happen is to know which are your superpowers and which are your pseudo-strengths.

The primary difference between superpowers and pseudo-strengths is how you *feel*. When you use a pseudo-strength, you feel drained. You feel less than stellar, lose energy and enthusiasm, and over time, you lose motivation to do the thing you can do so well. You may burn out, or worse, feel like you are having a nervous breakdown.

When you use a pseudo-strength, you feel drained. You feel less than stellar, lose energy and enthusiasm, and over time, you lose motivation to do the thing you can do so well.

My client "Sally" was the North American managing editor of an international news agency. With an office in Chicago and another in Times Square, her status couldn't go much higher. She was present during the shock-wave of 9-11 and despite knowing the Sears Tower across the street from her office was also a target, she remained at her desk and supported the staff on the ground in New York and D.C.

She continued to work throughout the aftermath, which proved to be dramatic and gut-wrenching. Anthrax attacks kept her journalist teams on edge. The position, it turns out, required too much of the wrong skill from Sally. The job was literally killing her and she left her position feeling like a failure.

Years and years later, Sally would hear stories of gratitude from those she managed. This helped to diminish the negative feeling and reset her perception that she failed. It also helped her re-frame why she left. "I can confess now, Lyn, I needed to leave because the role had me working from my pseudo-strengths." That's the point about pseudo-strengths. Other people perceive you are succeeding, yet you get worn down by the work. And, this is *big*, you feel weaker and drained because of your efforts instead of stronger and fulfilled.

It's easy to get trapped into a habit of relying on pseudo-strengths as a means to an end. Day in and day out there are things you and I need to do that ask us to use a pseudo-strength. For example, you may hate to cook, yet you are the main chef in your home. You get compliments about your meals, but the effort brings you little joy. Unless you have the means to delegate this chore to someone else, this will remain part of your role at home. You can cope with this situation because it is not your full-time job.

What we're looking for are things you do (at work and home) that are wearing you down. Massive amounts of time spent using a pseudo-strength steals the luster and joy from life. Take a moment and ponder where you might be working from a pseudo-strength and jot your ideas below:

WRESTLING WITH A PRETZEL

Now it's time to talk about weaknesses. Like strengths, we all have a weakness or two (or many), which you may be painfully aware of. A lot of people unwittingly believe that the way to be successful is to find a weakness and turn it into a strength. Nothing could be further from the truth, or a bigger waste of time and energy. The following quote from Harvard Business Review reveals that conventional leadership wisdom agrees. "No matter how hard you work on certain weaknesses, the logic goes, chances are you'll make only marginal progress. Don't waste too much time overcoming flaws; better to focus on what you do best and surround yourself with people who have complementary strengths."[1]

Gallup defines a weakness as "anything that gets in the way of your success."[2] Weaknesses definitely leave you feeling drained and even appear as "not your best work" to the outside observer. A long line of failures or misfires may indicate where you've been working from a weakness, proving it is not something that can be ignored. While we don't want to try to wrestle them into looking like a strength, we don't want them to constantly trip us up either.

The best thing to do with a weakness is to create a mitigation plan, or a system to manage it. I'm going to show you how to keep an eye on those pesky weaknesses later, so you have just such a system. For now, see if this example of my daughter's weakness brings one of your own to mind.

The best thing to do with a weakness is to create a mitigation plan, or a system to manage it.

I was horrified to hear my daughter's kindergarten teacher say, "Jessica's not going to make it in school." As a sixth-grade teacher at the same school, I witnessed my child excelling at social skills, organizational skills, problem solving, and figuring life out—a weakness hadn't entered my mind. Jessica's teacher was referring to her resistance to the things that public school systems require of children—sit down, focus on what I tell you to do, and then do it!

The system was not working for her and it left us both feeling weaker—she as a student and I as a parent. The next few years we experimented with alternative schooling such as Montessori and other private schools. Despite that first teacher's opinion, Jessica made it to high school just fine. There, she used her skills to devise a way to graduate early and exit the system. A success to be sure!

Today Jessica has many other successes under her belt. She's traveled the world, living and working in no fewer than 13 countries. She's sought-after by art departments and a bit of a MacGyver on movie sets. Jessica's movie credits can be found on IMDb.

Instead of wasting energy and time getting "good" at public school, Jessica put her effort into getting through school. She learned how to manage around the system and, in the process, invented her own pathway to success.

Your turn. What are one or more of your weaknesses— things you feel you need to mitigate? Again, we'll deal with what to do about them later. Make a simple list below.

_____

_____

_____

SUPERPOWER SEARCHING

Want to be super clear about what your superpowers are? Jump in.

Step One: Take as much time as you'd like to contemplate your answers to these questions:

List out a dozen things you can do that:

- make you feel like you're reaching a high level of excellence;
- you're enthused about and enriched by the activity;
- you can improve and get better at over time;
- you lose track of time when engaged in such activities.

Note that each of the items you list must meet all of the elements above.

_____

_____

_____

_____

Step Two: Enlist the help of a few people who have seen you in action over a considerable amount of time. They can be trusted co-workers, friends, or family.

Ask them:

- What am I doing when you think I reach a high level of excellence?
- When do you see me most enthused about doing an activity?
- What do I seem to get better at over time and you feel I'm on track to master this sort of action?
- When do you experience me deeply engaged and losing track of time?

Step Three: Compare your findings from both steps and from those you jotted down earlier in this chapter. If there are duplicate activities, tally how many times each one gets mentioned. Write down the "Top Five" things that are revealed by this exercise so far.

List them here:

_____

_____

_____

Step Four: Search through the list of 36 strengths offered up for resume building by Indeed.com. You can access the list on my book resources page, www.soulsalt.com/book.

Now add to your "Top Five" list but do not exceed twelve items.

Step Five: If you have already taken a strength-finding assessment, or some other assessment like it, and have your report, review it. A free version of Marcus Buckingham's Standout 2.0 assessment is also linked on my website at www.soulsalt.com/book.

Step Six: Allow your list of potential superpowers to grow to a <u>total</u> of fifteen. Then, narrow the list back down to five. What you are looking for are the five superpowers you currently use most often.

Remember to use this filter so that these five powers tick each box below.

When I use this superpower I:

- am completely absorbed and lose track of time;
- feel stronger and edified afterwards. I want to engage in something like this again;
- see myself getting better at this effort if I apply time and energy to it;
- sense something about the way I do this thing feels easy, like I'm in my zone;
- feel satisfied;
- feel capable and confident.

These five superpowers are ready for you write down as your own. Do that now.

_____

_____

_____

_____

_____

COMMON PITFALLS TO AVOID

I find that unless we purposefully utilize our superpowers for good, they can work against us. I wish I had a $100 bill for every client who came into my practice with an overzealous superpower. An overzealous superpower is one that acts like a weakness—or at least looks and feels that way to those around you. Robert E. Kaplan, who specializes in assessing leaders, warns that we must understand our strengths because they often get taken too far.[3]

Unless we purposefully utilize our superpowers for good, they can work against us.

A hypothetical example may look like a serial entrepreneur who has identified her superpower to be amazing vision. She gets so confident in this superpower that she tasks her team to figure out how to make her latest vision become a reality. Her task pays little attention to vetting ideas from her team before expending valuable resources.

An example of a person being used by their superpower is, a kind, good-natured employee finds he has a superpower of empathy. Instead of learning how to best manage this skill, he takes on the cares and concerns of everyone he works with. He develops ulcers and a difficult case of anxiety.

Pseudo-strengths can also "steal" time and energy from our superpowers. We have to use them unless there are employees, other team members, or someone else to take over these tasks. Albert Einstein warns us about being trapped in everyday habits that cause us to become numb and indifferent.[4] Be awake. Be aware. Don't let yourself become consumed with having a mediocre life. A pseudo-strength is the thief of time that could go toward a superpower.

One example of how a pseudo-strength may steal time from a superpower lies in a standard office scene. You can organize agendas and meetings better than most people in the office, so you become the default person for such tasks. But you standout when you lead meetings. Your superpower is inclusion and innovation when working with a small group of people. Instead of being productive and innovative using your superpower, you get stuck coordinating agendas and keeping meetings on track.

An example that happens in family or personal relationships is when one person has a pseudo-strength of being clean and organized. That person loves a clean room, always puts things away, and their closet and drawers are meticulously organized. This is done because it makes the person feel good and creates more sanity in their life. However, when a spouse, partner, or child sees the person doing this they may task the person to do it for them as well. The task actually drains the person when they have to do it for other people, so it's a strength that is using the person, not a person capitalizing on a superpower.

When coaching clients concerning their weaknesses, it is common to hear them say something like:

- "I hate it when I talk too much in meetings and gatherings. I am never going to do that again."

- "I have to stop procrastinating. Now!"

- "I want to completely end my habit of making quick decisions."

Have you said something similar? When it comes to managing weaknesses, it is easy to adopt the philosophy that total elimination is the best answer. Don't be fooled into thinking you can completely annihilate a weakness out of your life. That is a futile endeavor. Instead, transfer your energy into shrinking down the impact your weaknesses have.

Take for example the person who jumps to conclusions way too often. Our brains make assumptions and draw conclusions to detect threats. It's going to happen. Instead of trying to stop jumping to conclusions altogether, seek to have fewer instant reactions by inserting a pause. Train yourself to put a pause between a stimulus and the response. While your brain may still jump to a conclusion, and your body may still release chemicals that cause anxiety or stress, the pause will allow you time to move from the reactionary part of your brain to the executive part. Track this information in a notebook, or on your phone. Anything you track and put attention on will improve. Over time, you should see that your reaction time is increased and your conclusions yield more accurate results.

Don't be fooled into thinking you can completely annihilate a weakness out of your life. That is a futile endeavor.

Acceptance is big when it comes to managing your weaknesses. One of my clients had to accept that he consistently talked too much, or talked over other people. Once he accepted this as a weakness, he was able to create a system to lessen its impact. Now, he is training himself to count to ten before speaking. He's striving to make more space for others and to question his own motives. If he finds that his comments don't add value after counting to ten, he doesn't speak. There are still times when he can't help himself, but the frequency that his weakness causes damage is greatly reduced and he is much happier.

TAKE FIVE TO REVIEW AND CLARIFY

Just to review, everyone has superpowers, pseudo-strengths, and weaknesses. The key is to identify them for yourself. Your superpowers are literally the key to mastering your life. Putting focus and energy into them help you feel energized and joyful about what you do. Your pseudo-strengths can trick you into thinking they are superpowers when they are not. Just because you are good at something does not mean it is a superpower. To determine the difference requires you to note how you feel when you do an activity. You can't eliminate them completely, but the less time you spend using them, the more productive and happier you will be. Finally, be aware of your weaknesses and create a system to manage them. Don't let them keep tripping you up. They should not be the focus of a ton of attention, but ignore them at your own peril.

Superpowers, pseudo-strengths, and weaknesses are all important and you need to be aware of what they are. There is a place on the map to note your superpowers, and a "Caution Zone" to note your pseudo-strengths and weaknesses so they remain in your awareness. Superpowers are the most important for you to focus on and should be leveraged 75–90% of the time. Delegate where you can to avoid the trap your pseudo-strengths present. You may need to use them anywhere from 10–20% of the time—that's just the reality of life. Finally, shore up your weaknesses to get to a place where they don't trip you up on a daily basis. You're looking for progress, not perfection. You're seeking to decrease their effect. Don't go for total elimination of them since that is not possible.

TEST DRIVE THE NEWEST MEMBERS OF YOUR MAP

Record your superpowers, pseudo-strengths, and weaknesses in the back of this chapter. Then, you can reference it often and take action where needed. Don't beat yourself up if you slip back into a weakness or find yourself over-using a pseudo-strength. Acknowledge it and take a new action. The caution zone on your map can greatly help you mitigate spending time in areas that don't serve you. The executive I work with that identified talking too much as his weakness wrote, "*Stop talking. Start listening. Avoid talking over!*" in his caution zone. Another client whose weakness is overthinking decisions wrote, "*Make timely decisions. Determine what is necessary and go with that. Don't overthink it, just decide and move on.*" in their caution zone.

Remember, where your attention goes, energy flows, so reviewing your map often keeps you on the best path.

Okay, you're ready. Go out there and stay out of the caution zone as much as possible. Instead, explore what it feels like to live a week in the mighty shoes of your superhero self! You should be feeling proud of your accomplishments so far. You've uncovered some amazing Soul Salt about yourself that will serve you well. The next chapter will continue this trend by identifying some of the baggage we carry that isn't really ours, but we burden ourselves with it anyway. Grab your shovel, turn the page, and dig up some more great information about yourself that will guide you to your best life.

STRENGTHS

List up to 5 Superpowers Below:

1. _____

2. _____

3. _____

4. _____

5. _____

CAUTION ZONE

List 3 each—Pseudo-Strengths and Weaknesses

Pseudo-Strengths

1. _____

2. _____

3. _____

Weaknesses

1. _____

2. _____

3. _____

CHAPTER 6

Biological Baggage—We're All Full of Shit but Don't Know It

D o you have a foot that should be in a size nine shoe but you walk around in a toddler size five?

My grandchild wears toddler size seven shoes, so chances are if I tried to wear them all day the experience would be awkward at best. But, that's exactly what it's like when you walk around in a belief system you need to outgrow. Some of your beliefs aren't from you and don't fit who you are! Remember in the introduction when I told you that 95% of our beliefs and behaviors are hard-wired into our subconscious by age seven? Many of these beliefs and behaviors come from external sources when we were young, not our true self, yet we still "wear" them around like they are appropriate.

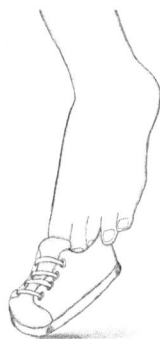

I have discovered two things from discussing beliefs and philosophies with my clients over the years. One, everyone I have worked with has at least a few lingering beliefs that were imprinted on them while they were young. When we discover what they are, we need to determine if that belief still serves them or not. More often than not, these beliefs are getting in the way of their desired progress. Two, it is rare, but I'm impressed when clients have identified one or two beliefs that they cultivated themselves as an adult. Whether they have stumbled upon the belief, or consciously chose it, the beliefs we cultivate when older tend to be more authentic. These beliefs help us move forward in life instead of hinder our progress. This chapter is all about helping you examine your beliefs and philosophies to be sure they belong to you.

> Whether they have stumbled upon the belief, or consciously chose it, the beliefs we cultivate when older tend to be more authentic.

THE "GOOD" AND "BAD" LABEL ROUTINE

Growing up, my parents insisted that there would be no caffeine in our home. Any drink that contained caffeine was labeled as "bad" and was totally off limits. That meant no coffee, no tea, no cola. Unfortunately, the label wasn't restricted to the beverage alone. Any individual seen drinking beverages with caffeine was similarly labeled as bad. Even while writing this paragraph, I smile and shake my head. I try to be compassionate to the child that was taught this ridiculous belief system because it created quite a conflict in my young brain.

You see, my beloved pseudo-grandparents who lived next door drank cola every day. And when they let me have a sip, I licked my lips and delighted in the carbonated goodness. I noted that nothing bad happened to me after drinking cola. These neighbors turned out to be some of the kindest, most giving people I would ever know. I never could see them as bad, so I side-stepped the requirement to stick that label to them.

Similarly, my favorite grandfather, Grandpa Morris, was a key factor in supporting me to go to college. He drank tea and coffee at breakfast every morning. Boy, was that aroma enticing. As I worked my way toward my degree, Grandpa Morris slipped me a spot of cash. I used this occasional gift to supplement a budget for books, tuition, or groceries. I am forever grateful for his generosity and foresight. His influence, my grit, and encouragement from a few other places had a long-lasting impact. This education eventually opened critical doors to my current sense of self. It paved a way for my professional role in society. Again, in my mind and heart, that "bad" label couldn't apply to my grandpa. So, I didn't try to make it. Not then. Not now.

Even with those experiences, it didn't stop the cartoon bubble with the word "bad" in it from popping up in my head when I saw someone crossing the street with a cup of coffee. The label was deeply ingrained from a belief that wasn't truly mine. It wasn't until I started enjoying a morning cup myself that this bubble burst. A new belief concerning the benefits of green tea, matcha, and the occasional cup of coffee took root. The ritual of the warmth and welcoming aromas have become a beautiful part of life. Thank goodness I could question, and keep questioning, beliefs like this. What seems even more ridiculous, however, is not checking our belief system to see if it serves us.

AT SOME POINT YOU HAVE TO QUESTION

Later in life, I hit a spot where the tiny shoe of "good and bad" labeling was squeezing too tight. It was cutting off my progress below the knees and wasn't serving me. Worse yet, holding on to the belief caused my coping skills to remain "too small" as well.

I found myself in a situation where I was being ridiculed, harassed, and even stalked. I instinctively reacted and labeled the perpetrators as bad. I felt justified considering myself good because I wasn't the one doing the harm. Well, that's not exactly true. I was harming myself by staying stuck in victim mode and not taking responsibility for getting out of a difficult situation. Why would I want to improve? My belief system required "bad guys" and "good guys." It allowed me to feel justified in complaining.

My boss, whom I respected, heard me ranting one day. He pointed out that I might want to look at the "unattractive chip forming on my shoulder." Boy, this comment smarted as it smacked me in the virtual butt. But I trusted him, which allowed the truth of his words to sink in.

Having "bad guys" and "good guys" in your beliefs allows you to feel justified in complaining.

He motivated me to do some personal growth and set self-improvement as my goal. Thanks to Karpman's Drama Triangle, a model of social human interaction, I learned to properly identify the roles of *rescuer, persecutor,* and *victim.* I learned the language of recovery and worked on boundaries and self-responsibility. This paraphrased passage from the *Tao Te Ching* encouraged me to move further from the label game, "A human illness is the need to label things as *good* and *bad.*" Eventually, I achieved my goal and replaced complaining with problem-solving.

Along with these lessons, I started questioning other beliefs on a regular basis. When I find something that doesn't belong in my adult life, or doesn't feel tenable, I work to replace it. I do this by seeking out beliefs and philosophies that expand rather than shrink. I cultivate beliefs that leave me willing to discover and be curious instead of trying to know so many things for certain. And, I am more apt to *include* versus *exclude*. It has been edifying, and quite a relief, to remove my feet from tiny, baby-sized shoes. After thirty years, this practice has added a richness to my life. There is room for trust and compassion to grow. More wisdom to guide and consult. And indeed, I enjoy more personal freedom.

Can you think of a time when have you questioned a belief system? What current belief might need some examination?

Write your thoughts below:

_____

_____

_____

SETTING THE STAGE FOR YOUR DISCOVERY

First, let's define beliefs as those things which you accept as true but cannot prove. For instance, over time I have formulated a belief in karma. I believe, but cannot prove, that what we put out comes back to us. When I find a lost wallet, I return it to the owner with the contents exactly as they were when it was lost.

> Beliefs as those things which you accept as true but cannot prove.

Next, consider what happens if we don't question our current beliefs. We may find prejudices, limited thinking, and biases have taken root. You may find you're not the person you want to be. Outdated beliefs cause us to misfire, or miss the mark when aiming at big targets worthy of the grown-up version of you. They cause our relationships to suffer, our professional trajectories sag, and a feeling of immaturity.

If you sense you need to separate from some of the beliefs you were raised with, this exercise is for you.

Remember back in Chapter 1 when I mentioned Dr. Robert Kegan's Theory of Adult Development? Kegan's theory breaks down adult development into the following 5 stages:[1]

Stage 1 — Impulsive mind (early childhood)

Stage 2 — Imperial mind (adolescence, 6% of adult population)

Stage 3 — Socialized mind (58% of the adult population)

Stage 4 — Self-Authoring mind (35% of the adult population)

Stage 5 — Self-Transforming mind (1% of the adult population)

When we go through life without examining our beliefs, we are stuck in Stage 3, where we care too much about what others around us believe and shape ourselves to fit in, or please others rather than be true to who we are. When we start to examine our beliefs and whether or not they are actually ours, we can move out of Stage 3 and toward Stage 4, the Self-Authoring Mind phase. You are headed there now!

Here are a few Stage 4 characteristics that indicate you are choosing a path, and belief system, for yourself:[2]

- We can question expectations and values, take stands, set limits, and solve problems with an independent frame of mind.

- We can explore other thoughts and feelings, creating our own sense of authority or voice.

- We can take responsibility for our own inner states and emotions.

  Example: "I feel angry because I interpret what you did as a violation of important values of mine, and if I interpreted your actions differently, I might feel sad instead."

- We generate our understanding of the world and are not unduly shaped by the context in which we find ourselves.

- We realize that we're always changing, that who we are is something that we can still negotiate.

Want a greater sense of direction? Separate yourself from the opinions and expectations of others. Use your energy to follow a self-made framework of beliefs. Shed what was imposed and engage what *you* have formulated.

Off the top of your head, write down two beliefs you know you formulated for yourself:

_____

_____

Now I want to shift gears a tiny bit and talk about belief's close cousin, philosophy. When referring to philosophies, consider your attitudes, or points of view. While strongly related to beliefs, philosophies tend to be more regular occurrences in your daily life. They're like frameworks you consistently live out that can apply to various areas of your life—from the practical to the ethical.

Here is a drawing of my personal 3x3 Philosophy of Productivity.

3 x 3 Philosophy of Productivity		
Relationship	Self	Work
• Susan -ritual -connection -partnership	• Fitness & Fencing	• Coaching -continual growth
• Family -support -connection -fun	• Nature & Gardening (dogs)	• Content -books, blogs speaking
• Friends -nurture & enjoy consistently	• Learning & Evolution	• Innovation -explore & expand

I know that I tend to over commit. So, I allow myself only three areas of focus. Within each area, I can have three sub-points. Once these nine spots fill up, I can't add anything more. If I do add something new, I must first take something off the chart. When/if I exceed this framework, my quality of life and progress suffer.

Take a moment and jot down one or more of your self-authored philosophies:

_____

_____

_____

Beliefs and philosophies are important for many reasons, but one of the most important is that we can anchor ourselves to them when dealing with change—which is constant here on planet earth. You may be feeling the need for change right now as you read this paragraph. The following are a couple of exercises I use to help clients make a leap forward.

UNDER THE MICROSCOPE

This exercise provides a method to examine if a belief belongs to you or not. I consider it putting a belief under the microscope.

Step One: Write the belief you want to examine.

_____

_____

_____

Step Two: Run the belief through the following questions to determine if it is still a good fit for you. Do so by answering with a simple "yes" or "no" answer.

1. Does the belief make it easier to make big life decisions?

2. Does the belief support me in pursuing my passions?

3. Does the belief benefit and grow healthy, long-term relationships?

4. Does this belief help me disengage from destructive thought patterns? Especially when things get tough?

5. Does it aid in offering me greater amounts of self-discipline or self-mastery?

6. Is it conducive to growing more harmony and flow between me and others?

7. Is this something I'd feel 100% comfortable sharing with others?

8. Does it expand my options versus limiting them?

9. Does it add to my development and growth more than keeping me stuck in one place?

10. In an ever-changing world, is this belief stabilizing?

Step Three: Add up how many times you answered "yes." If you had six or more "yes" answers, move on to Step Six. Otherwise, move to Step Four.

Step Four: If you had fewer than six "yes" answers, look at that belief again. How is it serving you? Is there just one thing you can tweak to get that belief in line with the "you" of today (or even who you'd like to be in the future)? What would that one tweak be? OR, do you need to exchange the small, undersized belief for a better fit?

Step Five: Write the new belief here and take it through the same ten questions above.

_____

_____

Revise your belief until you can achieve at least six "yes" answers. Then, move on to Step Six.

Step Six: Track yourself over a period of five days as you practice the new belief. Tweak and edit the new belief if you see fit, then ask yourself the following questions as the final test.

1. Does this belief result in better relationships and more harmony?

2. Does this belief give you reason to celebrate and enjoy life?

3. Does this belief open you up to share more of the good parts of you with others?

4. Does this belief afford you more appreciation and gratitude?

5. Does this belief expand your possibilities for goodness and grace?

6. Does this belief fuel your fire to discover more ways of being and believing?

If your belief scored a 6 out of 6, you have a winner that is fit to partner with you in finding the productive, joyful, meaningful parts of life. Wear it well. If not, keep tweaking it until the score is a 6 (or close enough that you feel good about claiming it). Repeat this exercise any time you feel it would support you, or you start to question if the belief still serves you.

RELEASE YOURSELF

Sometimes, if you aren't ready to work on a major belief, you can still free up energy and improve your life by releasing a smaller, limiting belief. There are countless limiting beliefs, but for our purposes I'll share the ten most common that I encounter with my clients:

1. Polarized "all or nothing" thinking

2. A fixed mindset

3. Forgetting to rest and reset
4. Getting stuck on how
5. Listening to naysayers
6. Self-criticism
7. Telling stories
8. Binary thinking: Right or wrong
9. Blaming others (and being a victim)
10. Everything I need to know, I've already learned

The following is a good exercise to do with an accountability partner to eliminate a limiting belief. You can work with a friend, a set of trusted peers or family members, your coach, mentor, or therapist.

Step One: Write down a limiting belief you want to change.

_____

_____

Step Two: Create a new belief that counters your limiting belief.

_____

_____

Step Three: Create a *Do More Of* / Do *Less Of* worksheet in a notebook, or download one from our website and track the limiting belief for two weeks. (Get the worksheet at www.SoulSalt.com/book)

The idea is to catch yourself using the old belief and track that by giving the belief you're trying to move away from a red dot. Then, you move to the right-hand side and tell yourself the new belief, then color in a green dot. Then go do an action that reinforces the new belief and color in an additional green dot.

DO LESS OF	DO MORE OF

I will do more _____ | I will do less _____

(Color with red) *(Color with green)*

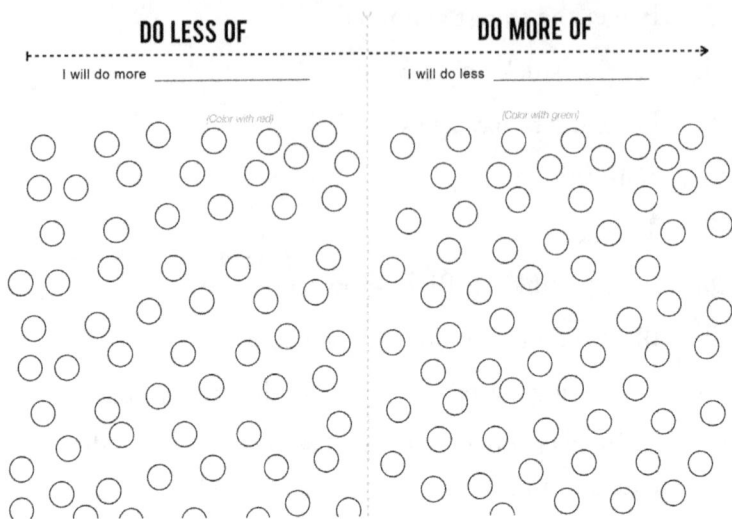

Over time you will shift the old belief into something more constructive and useful. We're not light switches so we can't just turn off a limiting belief and turn on a better belief. Have a little patience with yourself.

Step Four: After two weeks, report back to your accountability partner. Discuss what you've learned and ask them to point out when you are exhibiting the new belief. Keep the growth going as long as it seems beneficial.

LET'S CHART IT!

Once you have solidified at least one belief that is yours, write it in the back of this chapter. If you have discovered more than one belief, or wish to include an accompanying philosophy, add them as well. Things to consider as you do this:

- What beliefs and philosophies do you sense are most important at this moment?
- Which ones will be useful guides for this season of your life?
- Which beliefs and philosophies will add value if you reference them now and often?

COMMON MISTAKES TO AVOID

I certainly don't want you to be too hard on yourself as you allow your guide to direct your life. One way to be even-handed and wise is to keep a watchful eye on these three mistakes:

1. **Avoid the mistake of rushing through these exercises.** Go deep and enjoy the process. If a belief is an old one, it might require more patience. You may need more time to rewrite and replace it as well.

2. **Don't allow beliefs to conjure up hatred.** Don't get trapped in "othering" groups of people. Beliefs that do this fester inside you and make your life miserable.

3. **Believe in change.** Believe that your brain *can* modify after a certain age. As we age, learning and change may take longer and require more effort. Yet, you can still teach an old dog new tricks. Changing our brain at an older age means that once you get a concept, you own it. That new belief or knowledge will have more sticking power, even more than those you absorbed as a youngster.[3]

TAKEAWAYS

Not everything that guides your behaviors originated with you. We all have antiquated beliefs and philosophies playing in the background that make us stay small. You didn't cause this situation that we have been discussing, but you are key to solving it. Sorting through our belief system is helpful and freeing, like clearing out and reorganizing a refrigerator, a closet, or a messy drawer. It gives us new energy and places us in a self-authored status that feels empowering and impactful. The effort to address one's beliefs is a contributing factor to leaving a mark on this life in a way only you can.

Now that you've upgraded your belief system, even if only by a fraction, you've set yourself up for success. By putting yourself through the ringer of this chapter's offerings, you have expanded the field of possibilities for yourself. You have increased what is possible for the world and other humans living here with you. With that in mind, let's explore what some of these possibilities might be. I can't wait to show you what's next.

> *An unexamined faith is not worth having, for fundamentalism and uncritical certitude entail the rejection of one of the great human gifts: that of free will, of the liberty to make up our own minds based on evidence and tradition and reason.*

> —Jon Meacham

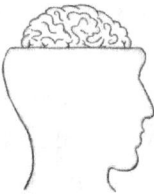 # BELIEFS

List 2 of Your Beliefs Below:

Belief 1:

_____

_____

Belief 2:

_____

_____

PHILOSOPHIES

Now list 2 Philosophies:

Philosophy 1:

_____

_____

Philosophy 2:

_____

_____

CHAPTER 7

The Cleverness of Possibility: What If Imagination Leads?

Tony raises his hand to pause the fencing match. Six feet apart, we lower our weapons. Tony pulls off his mask, so I follow his lead. He leans in and discretely says, "I'm beating you because I'm good. But just so you know, you should move your feet more. And you really need to watch your distance." I listen, trying to absorb his wise, free advice into my novice mind. I nod in silent assent, mask back up, and return to *en garde* before we go at it again.

Tony is eight. I am 58. He beats me soundly.

Granted, he's been fencing for years and I've attended three classes. But I find no shame in my position. In fact, I'm grateful to spar with someone who is willing to give me pointers. Starting as a novice inside the "youth" class is a safe place. It is an honorable beginning for learning a complicated, difficult sport.

Why am I putting myself through this? Why would I trade the podium in Sprint Triathlons and Spartan races for defeat at the hands of an eight-year-old? The first question I'll answer. The second question you can answer after you read more.

WHY AM I PUTTING MYSELF THROUGH THIS?

I've wanted to learn to fence since 6th grade. It started when my cousin, Paul, got a part in a play that required him to learn swordplay. I spotted what looked like a legit sword in his room one Sunday afternoon and asked about it. Paul explained that the sword was actually a *foil*. He went on to say how a foil was part of an Olympic sport called fencing. The revelation blew me away and part of my heart jumped out of my chest. I knew at that moment I wanted to learn to fence someday.

Think about a few things you might have on a "someday I want to . . ." list. Write them down below:

_____

_____

_____

Growing up in a small rural town did not afford me a chance to find a fencing program. But when I graduated and went to college, Paul gave me his foil and suggested I take a semester of fencing. I did, and the sport put its hooks into me. I wanted to learn to be better at the sport and vowed to belong to a fencing club someday.

Life got busy with a job, then marriage, then a family of my own. Every once in a while, over the course of nearly 40 years, I would spot the foil tucked in my closet and it would remind me of my dream. From time to time, I'd pull it out and mimic a move I learned in college. Then I'd put the weapon back in its place and promise myself again that, "someday, I'm going to learn to fence." It took decades, as you can see, but I did it. I made this possibility come alive.

It is hard to explain the gratification and zest for life one has when a long-held dream becomes a reality. The counter point is the frustration and downright depression that results from consistently ignoring our dreams. And that is the problem of placing your possibilities on the whim of "someday."

Possibilities = those things that could happen if we allow them.

Someday is not something I've ever found by turning a page in my planner. Have you? There is power in possibilities. There is power in persistence in keeping promises made to yourself. With a bit of patience, a dash of timing, and a pound or two of will, you can make those things that live in your heart a reality. You can make that *someday* happen.

There is power in persistence in keeping promises made to yourself.

Do you know what I call the system I use to make my dreams come true? I call it a *Possibility Practice.* I'm going to show you how to start one for yourself so you can create your own version of this miraculous practice. And, just in case you think such things are frivolous, take a lesson from the Make a Wish Foundation. They live in the possibility of wishes and dreams all day long. They know that some of the benefits of making a wish, a dream, or a possibility more tangible are:[1]

- Experiencing more positive emotions.

- Replacing fear with confidence.

- Moving anxiety out and replacing it with hope.

- Giving sadness the boot and making room for joy.

A Possibility Practice also activates your prefrontal cortex and the heart and gut networks— all those places where your wisdom and deep identity reside.

IT'S EASY, FUN, AND GOOD FOR YOU

Step One: Start with a blank sheet of paper and try recording your answers freehand. Old-fashioned note- taking is more effective than doing so on a digital device.[2] Working this way accesses the capacity of all three brains.[3] Who doesn't want that kind of power fueling your Possibility Practice?

Step Two: Answer the following questions:

1. If I could wish for the impossible, what would I want?

    _____

    _____

2. What adventures and activities intrigue me?

    _____

    _____

3. If I had all the time and resources I needed, and knew I would not fail, what would I want to make happen?

    _____

    _____

Step Three: Refer to your Values, Strengths, UPNs, and Beliefs/ Philosophies.

Pretend you have a magic wand. If these parts of you could ask you to grant them a wish, what would they each ask for? Write your responses here:

_____

_____

_____

Here's an example from one of my career reinvention clients. In this case she was working from a list of her superpowers: Inspirer, writer, and connector. Her superpowers "asked" her to speak to large audiences and get interviewed on podcasts to facilitate inspiring change in human interactions.

Step Four: Consider the aspirations that you have either spoken out loud, or held close to your chest. Use the following prompts to think about your aspirations. See if you can list up to ten items per prompt. That's right, stretch yourself. See if you can finish this step with sixty answers:

1. Things I want to do:

   _____

   _____

2. Places I want to visit:

   _____

   _____

3. Achievements I want to earn:

_____

_____

4. Items I want to own:

_____

_____

5. Ways I want to feel:

_____

_____

6. Experiences I want to have:

_____

_____

Step Five: Take a break. Go for a walk. Come back to this exercise tomorrow. Allow yourself space. I often find that taking a break freshens our perspective and new ideas will pop up in those spaces. When you're ready, come back and add more possibilities to your growing list.

Step Six: Look through all the answers you generated so far in this chapter. Create a master list of possibilities. Then, select one of your possibilities and place it at the back of this chapter. You can place up to two, but I caution against putting more than two.

NOW WHAT HAPPENS?

You have set yourself up for engaging in a Possibility Practice. A Possibility Practice is a pattern of listening to the intimations of the heart. It is a means of hearing them and honoring them. Whether you call them dreams, wishes, or possibilities, add them to your collection when they pop up. Even though some of the items on your list will never happen, the intention is that the most important *will* come true.

It may take time and practice to determine which items are which, but you have some say in this as well. When you place a possibility on your map, you are signaling that you intend for this thing to happen. It could become a goal, or it could be a signal you send out to the forces of nature asking for assistance to make it come true. The idea is that you find a way to make some of your dreams come true. And when you do, take notice.

Notice that you upgrade the sort of energy and vibrant positivity you experience. Notice the increase in personal excitement and engagement. This is one of the wonderful ways to invigorate your life. Your Reticular Activating System (RAS) is part of this process. It is part of your brain— specifically, a bundle of nerves found in the brain stem. It filters out unnecessary information. By doing so, it shines a "spotlight" on things you deem as important. That is why if you decide you like a particular style of shoe, handbag, or car, you start to see it all over the place. When we determine that a particular possibility is something you are zeroing in on, the RAS can help you. It can help you "see" and "hear" opportunities for it to occur.

But back to the Possibility Practice. Rather than describe it, this is one way it can look when activated:

YOU HAVE REALLY STARTED SOMETHING, LIKE SO MANY BEFORE YOU

I have a treasure trove of emails and other messages from clients reporting how their dreams have come true. They are a delight to read, and reread. Imagine the joy and contentment, the surprise and vitality the client experiences. A couple of my favorite success stories follow.

Cat

Cat lives in Oregon. She's an executive in the world of designing office space. I remember receiving a text the day after she added a specific aspiration to her guide. The text basically said, "Done! Not even twenty-four hours have passed, and this possibility came true. Just wanted you to know."

Heidi

Heidi is the owner of an extremely popular pre-school. I learned about her desire to visit Paris within the first two months of working with her. She told me, "I can't explain all the reasons why this is important to me, but it is. I took French as soon as it was offered in the 9th grade. I was only 15 and never thought my dream would ever happen. So, I didn't really even make it a goal. It always felt so out of reach. I had this trip on a dream board. I have Eiffel Tower pictures all over my house.

"Then one day my daughter, Mekall, who is a flight attendant, said she was close to quitting. While she was working for the airline, we had access to flight benefits. I realized we could use them to get to Paris, but the timing was not ideal. Thinking that if we didn't jump at this chance the opportunity would be gone forever, we jumped. It's easy to think you can't afford something, or you can't take the time. It's easy to feel too busy and prioritize work. But we went anyway, and guess what? It all worked out. When the trip took place, it looked different than I had dreamed it would. We flew on standby. We stayed in affordable hotels. We actually flew to London, rented a car, and ferried over to Paris. I got emotional walking up and seeing the Eiffel Tower once we finally arrived.

"And here's what I learned about possibility—I learned *anything* is possible. I have to remind myself of that. I have learned from this experience that I never have to believe something is out of reach. It is easy to say, 'I can't.' But that isn't true, is it? I have proof."

You can feel this way too and have what you desire! How would it feel to take the leap of faith toward one of your dreams like Heidi did? What you're feeling now is close to what Heidi felt. And it is something you can duplicate over and over. You can use this practice to inject massively positive vibes and experiences into your life.

Andrew

Finally, let's talk about Andrew, who I mentioned before. He experiences his best sense of self when he's writing. All day long Andrew uses his superpower to write copy and articles for those who employ his mighty skills, which can make it difficult to take time for your own stories and novels. But, after adjusting his schedule to keep this dream alive, Andrew did it. He recently left me a Marco Polo video explaining how he maneuvered a way to get personal writing time. He only gets two, 90-minute writing sessions a week for his own projects…if he's lucky. Yet, that has been enough to bring the heart-felt satisfaction he craves, and honestly, that he needs. Remember UPNs?

BUT WAIT, THERE'S MORE

Have you picked up on a few of the benefits of having a Possibility Practice? Guess what, there's more! Research indicates the act of honoring our hopes and dreams offers the following:[3]

- We are able to stay more positive over a longer span of time.

- We are more likely to increase our motivation and enthusiasm.

- We are less likely to suffer from dementia.

- Risk of death lowers when we have a hope and dream that we are seeking.

- We improve our overall brain function.

- We enliven ourselves and others when we have a possibility that we are pursuing.

I have seen evidence of each of these dynamics happening in the lives of clients who have this kind of practice, along with these additional benefits:

- Clients become more imaginative and creative in all areas of their lives.

- They ignite an element of passion and joy that no other activity seems to ignite.

- They experience healthy levels of dopamine and an increase of serotonin. Both of these neurochemicals contribute to a sense of positivity and a sense of inner peace.

- They feel a stabilization, which allows for more patience in the moment and joy in anticipation of the future.

If you're wondering what is possible for you, get cracking and find out, and keep an eye out for these common pitfalls.

THINGS TO WATCH OUT FOR

This is not an exhaustive list of pitfalls to watch out for, but it will get you started on strong footing.

1. **Avoid attaching the heaviness of personal responsibility to every possibility.** Just because you created the idea of a

possibility doesn't mean you have to commit to it. Allow that a big percentage of the things you write down won't ever materialize. That's okay. You won't have time, resources, energy, or even a real desire to do them all.

2. **Avoid thinking that listing out your possibilities is a one-and-done activity.** Many clients revisit the exercise in this chapter every 18 to 24 months. Some simply keep an ongoing collection process. The idea is to continually pay attention to the little and big heart-dreams that occur to you.

3. **Don't take your Possibility Practice too far by making it a list of goals.** That builds too much pressure and produces unnecessary judgement. Don't do that to these precious parts of you. Some of the items on the list will come to full realization once you acknowledge them, or once you clarify how much they mean to you. Other times, you may realize the possibility should be transitioned to a goal. In this case, remove it from your possibility practice and place it into a goal-getting system of some sort. Possibilities and goals need to be treated differently.

4. **Don't have too few items in your possibility collection.** Once upon a time, I received a challenge called the 100 Aspirations from my mentor, Judith E. Glaser. She asked me to take 30 days to see if I could come up with personal and professional aspirations and get to 100. Boy, did that stretch me.

I've had a Possibility Practice for as long as I can remember. However, I haven't always encouraged myself to allow "all things" to be on that list. When I accepted Judith's challenge, I did get to 100 in 32 days. And I can attest that you may miss the magic in your Possibility Practice if you limit yourself. If you don't allow for many, varied, and unusual amounts of ideas to flow, you'll pay a price. A price of less magic.

COMMON BELIEFS WE HAVE TO COUNTER

Some of us were not encouraged to dream big and wide. Some of us were encouraged to dream, but have developed beliefs and fears that hold us back. I am a strong advocate for you to have your deepest dreams permeate your life. It is palpable energy we're talking about. So, counter any and all of these beliefs if they are standing in your way.

Possibilities don't come true for me. Do you think you've tried things like this and they never work for you? If this is something you encounter, consider what your inner critic is trying to say. Is it trying to keep you safe? Is it afraid that if it grows too big with possibility it might distance you from others you care about? Listen to your head, heart, and gut. Sometimes the "negative nelly" voice is an old tape you can throw in the trash. Sometimes you just need to find a way to be safe and still go big.

A Possibility Practice is for airy-fairy folks, not for rational and practical thinkers. I know it sounds like this is a "soft" concept that could be categorized as airy-fairy, but it is based in neuroscience and quantum physics. Let's start with the quantum physics portion. Everything we encounter in this physical world of ours is made up of atoms. We learned this in third grade. When scientists look at atoms, what they find is that 99.99999999999 percent of an atom is empty space. Upon further inspection, scientists find that this space isn't exactly empty. It is a space filled with three things: information, energy, and potential. Every atom is a pool of possibility waiting to form into wonders and take shape into things we desire. This field of possibility is what scientists call the quantum field. You are made up of atoms; you hold the same amount of space for information, energy, and potential. You are a walking field of possibility!

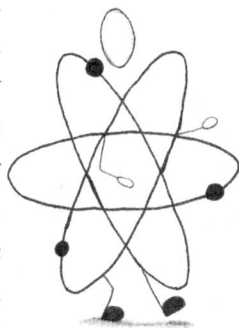

The neuroscience of possibility is such that it lights up the prefrontal cortex—the "executive" brain and highest functioning part. It also activates heart and gut neurons. In a way, you've activated that infinity sign of potential in your body within these brains. You can feel the electricity of potential when engaged in this practice. Believe in your own somatic experience; it's telling you that this is a healthy thing to do.

Finally, don't "should" yourself. Don't believe that you shouldn't be dreaming so big. You have just as much right as anyone else to all the great things life can offer. So don't buy into a belief that thinks otherwise!

SHORT AND SWEET

The short and sweet of this chapter is simple—you possess various facets of potential and possibility. Some of this wonderful potential lies in the dreams and hopes of your heart, the wonders of your mind, and in the instincts of your gut that you have a big and lovely life to lead. Engaging in a Possibility Practice is a simple way to activate all the elements of you, and the quantum field, to increase your chances of achieving your dreams.

While not every possibility you write down will come to fruition, a Possibility Practice definitely increases the likelihood that magic and wonder will visit your life more often. Next, adventures lie ahead in Chapter 8 where I provide another edifying experience that rides nicely on the coattails of your newly formed Possibility Practice.

POSSIBILITIES

List your top 5 possibilities below:

Possibility 1:

_____

_____

Possibility 2:

_____

_____

Possibility 3:

_____

_____

Possibility 4:

_____

_____

Possibility 5:

_____

_____

Define Your Own Success Metrics

The way person A "wins the day" may be too simple for person B. And the way person B defines success may be irrelevant to person C.

Unless you're playing a game of comparison, you don't want your neighbor's metrics for success to be yours too . . . do you? Absolutely not! You are the one who knows what you're trying to accomplish, so don't let others weigh in on how to measure your success. Even if you ignore their suggestions on what your success should look like, chances are slim that you've sat down and actually created a system to determine if you're moving in the right direction. One question I ask to every client is:

How are you defining success?

You're lucky if someone has asked you that, or if you had the insight to ask yourself. We typically measure our accomplishments in metrics:

How high?

How far?

How much?

How soon?

How good?

Until you comprehend that the number, letter, or whatever the metric is, doesn't mean a thing unless you say it does, you are blocked from living life on your own terms. Living a powerful life requires that we get crystal clear about what success looks like. Then, once you know, you must define your own success metrics and check in with them often. Let me show you how.

MEASURING SUCCESS

When it comes to defining what success means to you, I have two pieces of good news:

1. It's never too late to start defining it for yourself;

2. And, you are the ultimate authority. You get to say what success looks like and feels like. That is, in my book (and this is literally my book), exactly how things work best. You are the ultimate authority on your own success.

That doesn't mean it will be super easy. There will be times when you may be perplexed or anxious about doing it right, or doing it well. That's totally normal. Though you don't want to measure yourself against others, sometimes it is okay to see what they are doing to succeed and what they use as metrics. It can be especially useful when the thing you want to succeed at is something they've already accomplished. But here is my promise—the process of defining your own metric of success is one of the most gratifying and adult things you might ever do. You can do it. I know you can! All my clients have because I've broken the process down into bite-size steps.

> Until you comprehend that the number, letter, or whatever the metric is, doesn't mean a thing unless you say it does, you are blocked from living life on your own terms.

A FOUR-YEAR SUCCESS STORY

Take Angela, a dancer and former gymnast. After watching a woman win gold with an extremely athletic and strength-based pole performance, she saw that goal for herself. She immediately wanted to push her limits and be on stage performing and winning at competitions. It took four years of hard work and focus to walk away from an international competition with gold around her neck. But defining success for herself didn't stop with a medal.

Angela also acquired a business partner and opened up *Moxy Movement Studio* (a community where adults explore physical potential and build confidence through movement). To this day, 11 years later, Angela continues to compete, create unbelievable routines, teach, and support her students to win competitions as well.

I recently checked in and learned about her new definition of success:

"I now define my success in broader terms - like staying open and rebuilding through the pandemic times, by maintaining, nurturing and growing a studio and community that supports and creates together, through uplifting people to see themselves as more. My goals are broader in helping more people with

their health and wellbeing through pole and dance. And of course, I'm looking forward to new competitions too! "

Winning a gold medal may not be your cup of tea. Perhaps success for you means getting two 90-minute writing sessions in each week for three months. Maybe success is gracefully and confidently speaking your mind, regardless of the consequences. Along the way, you'll almost certainly meet people who will want to define success for you. But remember what Einstein mused, "We must keep choosing . . ." and this means choosing your own definition of success.

Look around and you'll see people mimicking their neighbors, their peers, and what they see on a screen. You see them chasing after a title, money, that shredded body, or social status as proof of success. Is that sort of success genuine and profitable? Not to say that these can't be valid indicators of success if that is what *your* head, heart, and gut say. But before you consult the latest trends for your cues, remember all the work we've done so far.

All this work has required you to go to your depths. You have made some bad-ass moves. You've left things behind and made tough choices. You have gained ground in knowing with greater clarity who you are. Now it's time to define how you determine what to achieve.

You're ready to define success for yourself. When you do, note how it invites in more happiness, satisfaction, and a stronger sense of self. Plus, it helps you find purpose. Spoiler alert—that topic is coming up soon in another chapter.

THE THING CALLED *SUCCESS*

Before you define success for yourself, it might be useful to understand its general definition. As Socrates said, "The beginning of wisdom is the definition of terms." Let's use the following general definition of success as a starting point to keep it simple—*the accomplishment of an aim or purpose.* The meaning of success will vary depending on what purpose, or aim, we are working towards. Ultimately, defining success requires two steps: stating your aim and stating an intention to determine when your aim hits that mark.

Here's an example of a client of mine defining success by stating her aim and intention. Elizabeth's aim was to have a difficult conversation with her business partner. The intended outcome in her words were, "I will be unshakable. No matter his response, I know my decision is right for me."

Do you see what Elizabeth did? She defined the completion of a small, yet meaningful, task as the mark of success. This is the beauty in having freedom to define success for yourself. You can assign it to something as simple as the completion of a few tasks. Or, you can define success for each day, or for an event. You can define it in terms of a week, a month, or a year. It's totally up to you!

Defining success requires two steps: stating your aim and stating an intention to determine when your aim hits that mark.

Jessica Gleim, who owns a marketing business, sculpted a multi-month metric to define her success. One of her *possibilities* was having a second child. She knew if that were to be possible, she would have to be able to leave work for two months to attend to her growing family—while not letting work consume her so she could enjoy the precious time. As she approached 40-years-old, Jessica got busy with her darling husband and got pregnant.

Checking in with Jessica after the fact, I received a positive report suggesting she was successful. Her newborn, Howie, is adorable and growing. Jessica spent an appropriate amount of time in bed, being cared for by her husband. Then, she transitioned into being a mom and dabbling at work as she saw fit. Things are good. Her metric for success continues to *flow*, as Jessica describes it, and she feels successful.

When I participated in my first Sprint Triathlon, I defined success as surviving the swim and finishing the race, no matter how long it took or what place I got. I challenged myself to compete in triathlons because at age 50, I hadn't learned to swim yet. After nearly drowning as a child, swimming petrified me. I challenged myself to compete in an XTERRA event to face off with my lifelong fear. I gave myself nine months to prepare, learn to swim, and get more fit.

To my surprise and delight, not only did I survive my first open swim in a reservoir, I won second in my age group. That win was all it took for me to redefine my success and spark a desire to compete again and again. My new metric of success was to maintain a high level of fitness and preparation. So, here's the measuring stick I created for myself:

I am fit enough to compete in a Sprint Triathlon on any given weekend in the summer and be happy, healthy, and not sore on Monday.

Don't limit your definition of success to task completion and goal acquisition. Consider a bigger perspective—what would success over a lifetime look like? That question is a bit more complicated and will take more consideration. However, I'm confident that once you complete the exercises that follow, you'll be ready to answer that **BIG** question.

QUICK PROMPTS

Let's warm up your skills for defining success by focusing on completing something small. Think of a task, a practice session, or anything relatively short in duration. Now, look over the quick prompts below and ask yourself:

- What am I going for?
- Why is this important?
- How does this align with items in my map?
- How will I know I've succeeded?
- What will I need to accomplish in order to feel successful?

Examples:

- I am successful if I can sink 50 putts in practice today.
- Success will be finishing this report in the next hour.
- I'll know I'm successful if I drop the mail at the post office; buy milk, bread, and cheese; and get the car filled with gas before I get home.

You're ready to decide how you'll measure success. Write that here:

_____

_____

_____

Now, go do the thing you said you wanted to complete. Make a note about your experience when you're finished below:

_____

_____

_____

START SMALL

Let's practice defining success for a bigger target. Define success for tomorrow, or for the weekend. Consider measuring the success of a short trip, or a presentation. Pick something slightly bigger than you did in the previous exercise and use the prompts below to expand your ideas for this new aim.

- What would your map say if it could define success in this instance?

- What would you need to do to finish and feel successful?

- What is your intended outcome? How can that outcome inform how you define success?

- What would you like to feel after you complete this endeavor? How can that feeling help you define success?

- In this case, what would success taste like?

- What have you done in the past in similar situations that can inform success this time around?

Determine how you're going to measure success. You may have discovered how by answering one of the prompts. Or, maybe an idea or memory occurred to you as you went through the prompts. Here are some examples if you are having a hard time:

- I win my day when I'm satisfied, ready to shut off my computer by 6:30 p.m., and have completed the two big items on my task list.

- I define success for tomorrow as getting my children picked up from school on time and making sure they are happy and have their homework finished before dinner.

- I am successful this weekend if my guests sparkle a little more as they leave my party than they did when they arrived.

Write your metric for success here:

_____

_____

_____

Now, go accomplish the event you've just worked on and celebrate your success when you achieve it! I'd love to hear about it on social media too. Post your success story and use the hashtag #soulsaltsuccess.

GO BIGGER, GO STRONGER

If you'd like more practice and feel ready to tackle something more substantial, try defining success for an entire area of your life. The idea is to narrow your focus to a particular area of your life such as:

- Health / Wellness
- Finances
- Romance and Relationships
- Environmental (Home, Community, National, Global)
- Emotional and Mental
- Professional
- Fun and Leisure

Write the area you chose to focus on here:

_____

Now, answer these questions with that area of focus in mind.

1. What will you have that you don't have now when your intention comes true?

_____

_____

2.   Who will you be when your idea of success becomes reality?

_____

_____

3.   What will you be able to do that you can't currently do when this thing actually occurs?

_____

_____

4.   What else came to mind as you worked through these questions that you'd like to add here?

_____

_____

Take note of the thoughts and emotions generated by your answers to these prompts. See if you can combine your ideas with your answers. From there, write a definition of success for this category of life.

Examples:

- I will have a greater sense of self and feel less impostor syndrome when I finally live in my own home. Success is having this feeling and being able to comfortably pay off my mortgage while enjoying my new space.

- I win when I am sitting on the beach in Hawaii with a cocktail in my hand and nothing to do for three days—no computer, no phone, no worries, no attachments. I just sit and make up what happens next from moment to moment.

- When my husband and I are closer and in greater harmony, I have more peace in my soul. Success is going through a week filled with joy, connection, and harmony.

Reflect on how this exercise went. What would you change? What went well? How would you use this strategy again? Repeat this process as often as you'd like.

_____

_____

_____

_____

DEFINING SUCCESS FOR A LIFETIME

I often appear on radio spots. One morning I sat with Frankie and Jess over at 97.1 KZHT, discussing the topic of measuring success. I learned that, similar to me, Jess defined one of her success metrics during a difficult moment in life. After moving from one school to another, Jess was teased and mistreated by many when she was young. She realized how much she valued good, loyal friends after she moved. Jess said, "Because I didn't have friends and I felt alone and teased all the time, I now measure success by the presence of strong friend connections and loyalty."

I related to this story because I only had three supportive friends during my coming-out season. So for both of us, we found a huge gap at a time of need. As we matured, we realized the value of what we didn't have and we turned that knowledge into a metric for success. One of my life success metrics is the desire to have people with open minds and soft hearts around me. This came from feeling the lack of such gifts during my coming-out season. You may already have some metrics defined to support your best life as well. But don't worry if you don't, I have an exercise that will help!

Let's take on the complex task of imagining what success looks like over your lifetime.

Step One: Take a moment and close your eyes. Imagine your life playing out exactly how you want it to. Take as long as you'd like. Use these prompts if they feel useful:

- Consider success within the various areas we discussed in the last exercise.

- Can you determine what you most hope to achieve in life?

- Think about how you want others to regard you.

- What is the main emotion you want people to have after interacting with you?

Step Two: Open your eyes and write your thoughts to these questions:

1. What does it look like when you've performed at your best within this life?

    _____

    _____

2. What characteristics have you embodied?

    _____

    _____

3. What accomplishments have you experienced?

    _____

    _____

4. Who are the people you've spent the most time with?

    _____

    _____

5. What are some of the habits and rituals you've cultivated?

_____

_____

6. What are your key relationships?

_____

_____

7. What has your career looked like?

_____

_____

8. What possessions are important to have within this lifetime?

_____

_____

9. How has your map played a role in guiding this life?

_____

_____

Step Three: Now take about 10 to 20 minutes to write down what you see for yourself in terms of defining success over a lifetime. Don't concern yourself with grammar or punctuation. Just list some of the milestones you seek in this life.

_____

_____

Step Four: Look at what you wrote and answer these questions:

- Do the goals and attributes you have written align with your values?

- Are these *your* intentions, or are these items based on the expectations of someone else?

- Do some of the things on your list matter more than others?

- Have you already accomplished some of the things on your list?

- If not, what are you doing now to work toward these outcomes?

- Would you change anything about your definition of success for a lifetime?

As an example, I share my own personal definitions below. I measure success with a lifetime view in three ways. Notice they are big, broad brushstrokes.

- I define success by how soft my heart remains and how open my mind is.

- I define success by how supported my family feels by me.

- I define success by how responsible I have been in living in alignment with my map.

As you can see, there are more powerful measures of success than dollar signs and accolades. For some, a definition of a successful life might be formulated by answering these questions:

- **Be True**: How and when do you speak and act from your soul?

- **Be Strong**: How will you express your strength and resilience?

- **Be Focused**: What are you pursuing when you know your actions truly matter?

Well done!

I know you have been working hard and you should be proud of this incredible accomplishment. It's a sign of success to be this far into the process. Take a second to record any and all of your definitions of success at the back of this chapter. Then, read on for a few words of caution when it comes to defining success. Perhaps they can help you avoid some common pitfalls.

WHAT TO WATCH OUT FOR

Don't let the object become the objective. Childhood conditioning influences how we view our success. Examples of this influence are when we jump through hoops to get bonuses, plaques on the wall, and fancy job titles. I'm not putting any of these accolades down—I myself have medals hanging on the wall in my office. They represent efforts made and challenges overcome. However, if you use a dollar sign, a position, or a piece of wood on your wall as part of your success metric, try to go deeper than the visual artifact. Consider the time, energy, and resources that you invested into those efforts. Emphasize personal growth. Highlight how you had to stretch your character. Let these objects be representative of something deeper rather than letting the object become the objective. Make sure the achievement is something you honestly care about. See if your "why" behind the "what" aligns with your map.

> *Make sure the achievement is something you honestly care about.*

Don't set your metric too easy ... or too hard. Think about the story of Goldilocks. Remember there are *too hard, too soft,* and *just right* designations for everything. Make sure you are challenged a bit when defining your success metric. You want it to stretch your growth so it's satisfying rather than just easy to reach. On the flip side, if we make the metric too soft, we dumb down our sense of self and become weaker. Set your success metric to be achievable while still requiring a bit of effort and this should be pretty close. Don't forget to call on your head, heart, and gut to help determine when the metric is just right.

Don't overwhelm yourself with this assignment. The idea is to make it a practice of setting your own standards of achievement. No one but you can be that authority. Since most of us were not taught how to do this, it can take time and practice. Keep at it and you'll improve your capacity. You'll become well-versed in setting your own effective and satisfying standards.

Don't let the outside world define success for you. It's perfectly acceptable to get external input, but be aware that socialization encourages you to accept others' definition of success. If you are more worried about getting it right, or what other people think, you may be stuck in a biased posture. Keep working until you know you have defined success in some measure on your own terms.

TAKEAWAYS

Success develops from your willingness to pursue a breakthrough. You are the person in the arena. You are the one fighting your own good fight. You are the one who knows the effort it takes to do what you do. You have earned the right and the responsibility to define success by your own terms. You may sweat all the way down until the salt of your soul spills out on the floor, but it will be on your terms.

Define success for yourself wherever it makes sense and as often as it serves you. Go deep, be true, and listen to your head, your heart, and your gut. By now you have proven that you know how to define metrics of success for yourself. Don't let anyone, or any situation, take that from you.

May the salt of your soul lead you to accomplish all of the great feats you set for yourself. I have confidence that you'll also succeed at the next adventure. Turn the page and let's see.

"Success means doing the best we can with what we have. Success is the doing, not the getting; in the trying, not the triumph. Success is a personal standard, reaching for the highest that is in us, becoming all that we can be."

—Zig Zigler

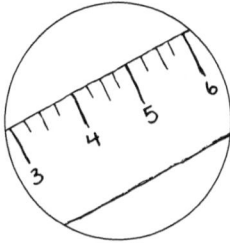

List 3 Success Metrics below:

Success Metric 1:

_____

_____

Success Metric 2:

_____

_____

Success Metric 3:

_____

_____

CHAPTER 9

Warm Yourself by a Fire You Didn't Start

Imagine being outside in the winter and the clothing you're wearing isn't warm enough. Imagine how wonderful and uplifting it might feel to be invited to sit by a campfire. Or even better, to enter a shelter and sit by someone's fireplace. Even if you didn't build the fire yourself, you were able to benefit from its warmth. This same concept is true about tapping into external sparks of motivation to keep you inspired and moving with positive momentum.

The goal of this chapter is for you to identify a few bits of inspiration that come from others and use them to inspire and warm you when you go through challenges or lose your motivation. Of course, there will be an exercise to help you gather your thoughts about these sparks and I'll have you plot them on your map to serve as banners of hope and support. But first, let me explain a little about how these small, but powerful, embers can offer you direction when you need it most.

YOU DIDN'T START THE FIRE

Up to this point, I've been asking you to look within to find your own answers. I know this can be frustrating, especially if you picked this book up hoping it would give you answers! But I challenge you this way because I believe that the bedrock, essential identity of who you are, is only found when something resonates with you. Specifically, when something aligns with your head, heart, and your gut.

What resonates with you doesn't have to come from inside. It's completely possible to be moved by the words, actions, or creations of another. Something as simple as song lyrics, or a verse from a poem can make your heart swell. A quote may shoot truth through your soul because you understand and embody the sentiment. Even images or meme's can be meaningful enough to jump-start a paradigm shift. In all of these cases, you may not have written the words, but you felt the message and resonated with the meaning. You were warmed by a fire you didn't start.

I believe that the bedrock, essential identity of who you are, is only found when something resonates with you.

This is a fairly universal reaction to these small bursts of inspiration. They impact us. So much so that countless clients report these stimuli leave them with:

a tiny spark of wisdom

a small dose of insight

a shot of motivation

a burst of affirmation

a flash of direction

a boost of reinforcement

Why does this happen? There are many reasons, some more scientific than others, but I will give you a jumping-off point. For one thing, song lyrics, an inspiring quote, and a powerful image are all telling a story that touches something familiar and stimulating to us personally. Our brains are wired to sync up with the narrative and feel the parts that are common to us. Areas of emotion (a heart modality) and movement (a gut modality) are activated. Additionally, functional MRI scans show various areas of the brain "light up" when we listen to a story.

Melanie Green, a communications professor from the University of Buffalo, studies the power of narrative. "Solid information of any form is good. But that's not necessarily enough. A vivid story can give that extra push to make it feel more real or more important." Consider those times when your mind, your beliefs, or your heart has been changed. Green says it's often because some parts of a narrative "hit them in the heart."[1]

Hearing personal narratives, even short ones like quotes and memes, cause our motivation and energy to increase, helping us stay the course. Kendall Haven, an internationally recognized expert on storytelling and author of *Story Proof* and *Story Smart*, wrote, "Information alone rarely changes current attitudes, belief, knowledge, and behavior. Research confirms that well-designed stories are the most effective vehicle for exerting this influence."[2] The following stories from my clients further confirm how impactful an external spark can be.

My client Lo, who is seeking career reinvention, was moved by the lyrics of the song *Closer*, by Slow Magic. She texted, " . . . this song moves me in a way that's different . . . chills running over my body, tears welling up—all the things you want a song to do. The subtle build to the finished effect, the ebbs and flows of the sounds, the highs and lows . . . it feels like me. So many layers to my metamorphosis over the last 6 months feel like this song . . . you can hear this growth and evolution through additions, withdrawals, and level changes. It leaves me in a place of believing it has more to give . . . I have more to give."

Another client of mine, Upuia Sagapolu, felt her heart sing when she read the following quote from the late congressman, John Lewis, "Never let anyone, any person or any force, dampen, dim or diminish your light." Her heart felt every single word of this message like it was written just for her.

My client Melissa is a gregarious, exciting, and dynamic leader. She oversees client partnerships within a software start-up. One evening she watched *Ted Lasso* on Apple TV, a show that follows an American football coach somewhat accidentally assigned to coach a British soccer team. She saw Ted give a short lecture to his team and then place a homemade "believe" sign above the door of the team locker room. Melissa went to her desk and designed a "believe" sign of her own and placed it over the door in her office. I see it every Zoom meeting as does her nation-wide team.

My Own Inspiration

My client Alexa was commissioned by the Jung Society to design a t-shirt and had given me one. When my partner, Susan, saw the message on the shirt her heart jumped. It was a quote by Carl Jung stating, "The privilege of a lifetime is to become who you truly are." She knew in an instant that this quote resonated with her life purpose. (Spoiler alert: we'll be talking about your life purpose in the next chapter.) In a few simple words, Jung lifted her spirit and both lightened and quickened her footsteps forward. Susan had a large copy of the quote printed and posted in her office where she sees it daily, and it is an important part of her personal map.

"Never let anyone, any person or any force,
dampen, dim or diminish your light."

—John Lewis, Congressman

Finally, I received the fire I needed when I read Theodore Roosevelt's "Citizenship in a Republic" speech—just as I felt a chill of self-doubt. Delivered in Paris on April 23, 1910, it is also known as, "The Man in the Arena." The passage which made the speech famous (and my soul burst into flames) follows. I have taken some liberty to make it fit me and those I work with.

> *"It is not the critic who counts: not the person who points out how the strong one stumbles, or where the doer of deeds could have done them better. The credit belongs to the person who is actually in the arena, whose face is marred by dust and sweat and blood; who strives valiantly; who errs, who comes short again and again, because there is no effort without error and shortcoming; but who does actually strive to do the deeds; who knows great enthusiasms, the great devotions; who spends oneself in a worthy cause; who at the best knows in the end the triumph of high achievement, and who at the worst, if they fail, at least they fail while daring greatly, that their place shall never be with those cold and timid souls who neither know victory nor defeat."*

The moment I read this passage I felt validated. I recalled years of weekends and nights spent working on building my business while other people were out on the dance floor, in pubs, and at movies. Even though I felt that I was being called to my true purpose, there were times when I would ask myself if my hard work and sacrifice were really going to be worth it. But at my core, I was willing to dare greatly. I didn't give up. Instead, I gave time, energy, focus, and strength to my dream. Perhaps this is one reason I am unshakably dedicated to helping you achieve your dreams.

Today, I use this piece by Roosevelt as a filter. If a potential client isn't willing to be that person in the arena of their own making, I'm not the right coach for them. My clients are either in the arena, or they are not my clients.

How often do you feel weary and need some wind under your wings or a spark in your step? What notion, idea, or work from another proved to be exactly what you needed in a particular moment? Get ready to recount a "fire" you didn't start that has warmed your soul.

TIME TO FIND YOUR CAMPFIRE

Now it's your turn to gather memes, poems, lyrics, images, and stories that shoot an arrow straight to your heart—fires started by others that spark something in you. They are the messages that give you hope, meaning, inspiration, and even direction. If you don't already have a collection of such, go on a scavenger hunt. Here is a list of ways my clients and I have found bits of inspiration:

- Go back to the exercise you did in Chapter 3 where you identified people you admire and respect. What is something they said that speaks to your heart?

- Pick one of your current UPNs and search for quotes on this topic. For example, if you need more courage, you might search, "courage quotes."

- Think about some of your favorite songs. Are there lyrics that feel like they were written for you? If so, do they seem like something you could use as encouragement or a piece of inspiration right now?

- Sit quietly with your eyes closed for at least 60 seconds and ask to be guided. Ask to hear, see, or read a message that will give you the spark you need/want most. Once the minute is over, stay aware and accessible to what shows up for you. Sometimes it takes a day or so for this method to work, so be patient and keep asking.

- Scroll through social media posts. Use hashtags to find quotes, memes, and words of wisdom on topics of interest to you.

- Read a lot. Read books, magazines, articles, and blogs for inspiration. Be on the lookout for quotes, phrases, and even single sentences that stoke a fire within you. This is great to do after sitting quietly and asking for guidance.

Once you feel you have at least one spark that warms you, write it at the back of this chapter. Later, you'll plot it on your map in the "Sparks of Inspiration" section.

BEWARE OF THE PITFALLS

Take care to avoid these pitfalls when searching for outside inspiration:

Don't wait to write them down. Capture these sparks when they first fly your way. It is easy to lose track, forget, or not be able to find that spark again if you don't take note of it in the moment. Capture it immediately and hold it dear until you can safely place it where it belongs on your map.

The spark doesn't have to be "perfect". Don't get trapped into thinking that you have to find that one perfect poem or quote that exactly resonates with you and every aspect of your life. Seasons of life require that we evolve, and as we do, yesterday's inspiration may fade. So, stay on the lookout and keep a list in a file, folder, or even a jar to preserve your sparks for when you need them.

Don't limit your fire-starters. Some folks find one statement for their map, others find many. Don't judge how many you "must" have. It is, after all, *your* map. So pick the number you need to stay inspired.

Don't isolate them to just your map. Feel free to post your sparks wherever you will regularly see them and get inspired by them. Put them on a mirror, in your car, on your computer. Let them flow to you and place them wherever you see fit.

DON'T GET IN YOUR HEAD

Think utilizing other people's words for inspiration is all hogwash? Studies out of Penn State University found that viewing Online memes increases confidence. It also increases your ability to have positive emotions and peace of mind. It can help you to experience less stress.[3] Someone else may be more capable of delivering the words you yourself would never have come up with—and didn't know you needed. They can give us what we need to be inspired. While I do encourage you to listen to yourself, I also encourage you to pay attention to the firing of your neural networks. When your head, heart, and gut recognize truth coming from an outside source, honor their wisdom and believe in your somatic response.

Post your sparks wherever you will regularly see them and get inspired by them.

Author Martha Grimes once said, "We don't know who we are until we see what we can do." I use her words often with my career reinvention clients. They need to see themselves through the eyes of their witnesses. Take a note from these clients and let yourself see parts of you reflected back through another's words.

There will be times in your journey when you'll feel like you don't know who you are, or if what you're doing is enough, or worthy. Then you'll hear someone speaking words that perfectly affirm your position. When this happens, accept the validity in those words. Let them sink in. If they take root in your soul, then they belong to you.

TAKE THIS WITH YOU

We've all sat by a fire we didn't start and found value, warmth, and energizing inspiration. This is a good thing. Allow yourself to notice what inspires you. In Middle English, the word inspiration means, "a sense of divine guidance." In Old French the word inspiration derives from the Latin word *inspirare*, which means, "to breathe or blow into." We can find both guidance and comfort when words touch us with hope and breathe new life into us. Like fires built by strangers we find along our journey, let the bits of inspiration you identified warm you, and be there for you when you need them most.

Experience how it feels to be seen, heard, and understood through the creation of another person. Be it a quote, song, poem, meme, or whatever inspiration you find, let it energize you. Then when you're ready, start the next chapter with your newfound vital energy. Be ready. Be willing. Next, we dive into the lofty yet lucrative effort of clarifying purpose—*your* purpose.

INSPIRATION

List 3 Sparks of Inspiration below:

Spark 1:

_____

_____

_____

Spark 2:

_____

_____

_____

Spark 3:

_____

_____

_____

CHAPTER 10

No Posers–Just Purpose

What do you think is happening in this cartoon?

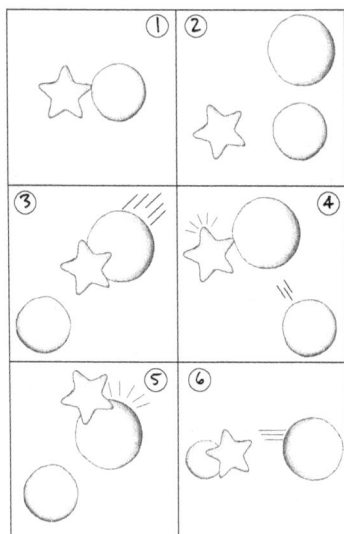

H umans naturally assign meaning to things, even when it's not given. Since you were not told the meaning of this cartoon, most of you likely conjured a story of your own. This is because in the absence of information our brains will make things up. It's the same mechanism responsible for those times when we jump to conclusions and is why we make assumptions. Our brain doesn't like a vacuum, so in the absence of information, it fills the void.

Psychologists Fritz Heider and Marianne Simmel created a 90-second animated film in 1944. Similar to my cartoon, it depicts two triangles and a circle moving around a box. Subjects who viewed the film attributed human characteristics and behaviors to the objects. If you could see a story in the cartoon, that is what your brain did.[1]

If you didn't make up a story based on the cartoon, don't sweat it. Some of you with logical and analytical superpowers won't "see" a story. Your sense of the cartoon will be more objective. You may simply notice that shapes and lines change positions in each frame. Regardless of which camp you fall into, I want you to know that there is no single "correct" meaning to the cartoon. There is no right answer. There is only the truth of what happened for you when you viewed it.

Assigning meaning to all sorts of things in life is normal. What is rare is to ponder bigger voids of information, like the meaning of life. No, I don't mean you need to answer the big question of the meaning of all life. According to Viktor Frankl, "what matters is not the meaning of life in general but rather the specific meaning of a person's life at a given moment."[2] So this chapter will focus on the question, what is the meaning of *your* life? As your coach and advocate, I'm hoping I've prepared you to look within yourself for answers and that you feel ready to at least *start* to the answer this question.

YOUR LIFE'S PURPOSE

This book started by discussing early programming from other people's expectations. We talked about how outside influences molded your young mind. These expectations and belief systems can give us something to aim toward and people to admire. So, in this way they can serve a purpose.

Sometimes, however, these beliefs blind us from seeing our own true path. They can make you feel like you aren't really in charge of your life, or where you want to be. This is because you are following someone else's vision of who you are and what you are here to do. What we're talking about here is *your* unique purpose—the one written in the salt of your soul—not what your family, community, or religion says is your purpose.

> Our brain doesn't like a vacuum, so in the absence of information, it fills the void.

The truth is, very few people have a strong sense of their own purpose and even fewer have a clear purpose statement that easily translates into action. In this chapter, I will coach you through developing a purpose statement which will help you further hone the next steps on your journey.

CRAFT A PURPOSE STATEMENT

If you have always felt in your heart that you were born to do something special, I agree with your heart. I believe you have something uniquely meaningful to do with your life, which is a great reason why you'd want to have a concrete statement of your purpose. In fact, there are many reasons. When we have a sense of our own purpose, we have an increase in hope, optimism, and resilience. But there's even more to it than those rich and desirable benefits. When you have a strong sense of your own purpose you tend to have:[3]

- More Joy, happiness, and satisfaction
- Better physical health
- A lower risk of death
- More engagement when studying something
- More enjoyment of the learning process

- A greater sense of belonging
- An increase in career satisfaction
- Greater leadership tendencies at work
- Increased income

All good things, right?

But here is where things can get tricky. Our mind feels safer when it knows the reason and purpose of things. It likes to know the "why". All too often we talk about purpose in a tone of reverence, like some all-knowing being must dub us with it in a ceremony.

Sure, you probably sense the importance of knowing your purpose. You may even believe that each soul has a singular purpose. But be careful to not make the picture so big that you create an image of some mystical, eternal reason for being here. If that kind of belief pattern gives you tension in your chest like it does me, just take a deep breath and relax.

There is no Holy Grail of purpose.

There will be purposes that come and go. There may or may not be an overarching purpose for your entire life. In fact, if all you desire is to assign a purpose to the smaller parts of life, like taking a family vacation, or living in a certain geographic area, or deciding to take a particular job, then that's perfectly okay! Nobody gets to tell you what your purpose is, or how and where to define it for yourself. Instead, I'm proposing an approach where you don't rely on external voices—and you won't have to chase after a mysterious relic.

Instead, think of our work on this aspect more like an archaeological dig—sort of like we conducted in the core values chapter. We're about to go on an expedition through the topography of the map you've already crafted. You're going to have a chance to assign purpose to your life in a unique and authentic way. In fact, you will get to pick from a variety of ways to excavate your purpose.

We'll start by determining purpose in the small, inconsequential areas of your life. Then, we'll go wider by reviewing the pieces of your identity you've already uncovered in this book for clues.

LET'S START SMALL

Like the exercise you did when defining success, start by picking a small project or event you have on your plate. This could be a house project, party, weekend getaway, or a night of movies and popcorn. Go ahead and decide where to practice your skills at determining purpose.

Write the thing below:

_____

_____

Now you need to determine your answers to these questions:

1. *Why am I doing this thing?*

_____

_____

2. *How do I describe its importance?*

_____

_____

3. *What moves me to complete this endeavor?*

_____

_____

With your answers to these questions in mind, take a crack at writing up a single sentence that expresses your purpose behind doing this one thing.

_____

_____

_____

How did that go?

Chat with a friend or confidant and discuss what you learned or experienced from this simple exercise. If you feel ready to start tackling bigger topics, including your life's purpose, read on. If not, play around with the previous section for a while. Repeat the steps above a few more times. Practice identifying your purpose behind many more small projects, then come back to this section.

LET'S GO BIGGER

Let's have a go at crafting a single sentence that explains part, if not all, of your life's purpose. I know, that is a lofty goal. But I don't expect you to get it right ("right" in the sense that it resonates completely with you) this first time out. Then again, what you come up with may surprise you. It may fit you perfectly and be elegant in its simplicity. And to be clear, when talking about your life's purpose I mean the reason behind the things you create or the things you do. **A *life purpose* helps explain a reason for why you exist.**

As you begin to excavate your own purpose, keep in mind that there is no one right way to uncover your purpose. I've provided three of my favorites here, starting with the shortest and most simple formula:

Method 1: Simple Formula

Step 1 - Answer the following questions:

What is the most incredible power inside you?

_____

What is the purpose of this power?

_____

What do you hope to do in order to fulfill or use this power?

_____

Step 2 - Read your answers aloud. Share them with a friend or confidant, if you like. Notice the thoughts, remarks, and feelings that come up while you share.

Step 3 - Write a one-to-three-sentence statement of your life's purpose here:

_____

_____

_____

How does that feel? Does it seem like you have a first draft, something to start with that can be edited and tweaked along the way? If so, you've done it! You have a statement that can now live and breathe in its honorable spot on your map. Place it there. If not, try the other exercises in this chapter. Try them all. Try on various statements to find a fit.

One client came up with the following three statements, each derived from a different exercise:

My purpose is to be a life-long learner. My learning and subsequent personal development will spill over and be a positive force for myself and others.

I am here to support others. It doesn't matter where or when. I help other people whenever it is needed.

Taking a stand for science and nature is my greatest purpose.

Method 2: Use Established Assessments for Help

Once upon a time when I was a teacher, I attended a leadership development seminar. I took a DISC assessment (a behavioral self-assessment tool based on the 1928 DISC emotional and behavioral theory of psychologist William Moulton Marston). My results indicated that the "S" or steady part of my nature was the strongest at that time. My second highest score was "I," which stands for being an inspirational sort of person. I pondered the information from this exercise. What circulated through my thoughts and feelings the most was a single statement: *You are a person who seeks peace and harmony. You also enjoy teamwork.*

It took some time to consider what this might mean. I wondered about my motivations. What did I want to do with my life? What did I want to create? Who did I want to be? I mulled over the question, *"If I seek peace and harmony and gravitate toward teamwork, what does this say about my life's purpose?"*

After about a week, a purpose statement slowly but surely cropped up. When it first played across my mind, my heart skipped a beat. My gut felt calm and in concert with the heart. That's how I knew it fit me.

I am an agent for goodness.

Since that time, I've scoured various assessments and survey results. Sometime after turning fifty, I took Marcus Buckingham's StandOut assessment. On page two, the report combined my top two strengths into a single paragraph: *You came here to enliven and enlarge people's vision of who they are and what they can achieve.* As I read this line, my head, heart, and gut started waving flags and giving me signals. They wanted me to know that I had been "seen" and "understood" and given words to describe my own purpose.

Scenes and actions I had taken, and decisions I had made throughout adolescence into adulthood played through my memory. This was indeed a mirror. From it, I could see part of my purpose. This statement is now part of my map.

Another purpose statement of mine is, "*I am here to enliven and enlarge your vision of who you are and what you can achieve because of who you are.*"

Writing this book is one part of fulfilling my purpose. If you want to follow suit and use this method to craft a life purpose statement, here are a few steps to take:

Step 1 – Review pages of assessments you've taken in the past (DISC, INTJ, career aptitude, etc). Add any documents that might also carry life purpose themes such as surveys or thank you notes. Also, consider answers you've given to other assignments in this book.

Notice if any one or two sentences jump out at you as potential statements of your purpose. If so, jot these down.

_____

_____

Step 2 – What did you find yourself doing as a child? When did you seem to be in flow and time flew by? What activities left you exhilarated? Write about these moments here:

_____

_____

Step 3 – Notice any commonalities within the items you just listed. Do you see duplicates? If so, note what these are:

_____

_____

Step 4 - Using your answers from above, craft a single-sentence purpose statement:

_____

_____

_____

This exercise works well for many, but not all of my clients. If you sense you would like a different approach, keep reading.

Method 3: Seven Answers to Purpose

This exercise should take ten to twenty minutes but may take more. Be sure to give yourself enough time. Answer the following questions:

1. What would you do if you never had to earn another dollar? (In case you're imaging Mai Tais on the beach, that's fine. Just imagine what you'd do after the monotony of that hits you.) Another way to think of this is, what would you do with your time if you still had an income but no day job to answer to? What would you learn or create? Where would you go?

   _____

   _____

2. What makes you so mad that you'll argue with a complete stranger? What are the topics? When friends bring up something that makes you angry, what do you want to do? What do you want to yell out loud?

   _____

   _____

3. What do you love? What interests are you emotionally engaged with?

_____

_____

4. What would you choose to do, even if it was difficult?

_____

_____

5. What did you love doing as a kid?

_____

_____

6. What makes you afraid of being judged?

_____

_____

7. What is the vision you hold of yourself that includes doing bold, fearless things?

_____

_____

Refer to your answers from above. Craft one to three statements that feel like good candidates for a purpose statement.

_____

_____

_____

Spend a day living true to each statement to test drive them. Let them have a turn guiding you through a day. Once you finish that experimentation, notice if you want to combine or delete any of these statements. Which statement/statements felt stronger and more fitting than the rest? Add one or more to your map if that feels correct and true to you.

REFINE WITH YOUR BOARD OF PEERS

Select three to five people to be on your temporary board of peers. Share a copy of your map with these folks and ask them the following questions:

1. What do you think I'm most interested in doing with my life?

2. Where do you sense I have made the most impact?

3. If you were writing up a purpose statement for my life, what would you say it should include?

Take the answers you capture from these conversations and mull them over. Write down the most recurring words and phrases or tally up the recurring patterns within the words and phrases of the responses. Using these frequently used words and phrases, fine tune your purpose statement.

Write the updated statement here:

_____

_____

_____

_____

PHEW!

I know that is a lot. But your life's purpose is a big damn deal. No matter if you used these exercises or some other method, place at least one draft of a purpose statement on your map.

Examples of Purpose Statements

If you have worked with me personally, or have interacted with my company, you have almost certainly met Shannon Dee. Shannon and I first met while I was the director at the Franklin Covey Coaching division. I was interviewing her and she shared that her purpose was "to help people." That purpose has transformed over the years and today it reads like this:

> *"I am here to contribute to the world's peace and harmony by raising a family of members that are also contributors to that same purpose. We lift the fallen and less fortunate. We support them as they carry heavy burdens by showing love, acceptance, grace, and inclusion."*

Being on purpose for architect Aaron Hansen is matching his architecture to the needs and dreams of his clients. Just recently, he created this purpose statement:

> *"To design custom homes and renovations for individuals and families, enabling them to cultivate their most meaningful relationships."*

John Schmidt, PhD, Chief Technology Officer, Zartico defines his purpose this way:

> *"I desire to be the leader and mentor that I never had. I have strong ideas about what kind of engineering organization I want to be a part of and I'm creating that."*

Judy Morris, the Chief Human Resources Officer at Progrexion, visualizes her purpose statement through an image. She sent me the picture below that reminds her of her purpose, which she explains is a balanced proposition represented by a three-wheeled bike.

BALANCE

1) GENEROSITY
2) COURAGE
3) ADVOCACY

Her statement reads:

> *"My purpose is to help people feel safe, stop hurting, find their voice, feel empowered, and experience the fullness of life. I will do this through the following three principles:*
>
> *Generous — Because I have far more than my fair share.*
>
> *Courage — Required to set hard goals, push yourself, be vulnerable out loud.*
>
> *Advocate for others — See the need and make it a priority. Do the job without judgement"*

COMMON MISTAKES TO AVOID

Drafting a purpose statement can be daunting and satisfying all at once. To help you on this strong journey of self-authorship, watch out for some of the top mistakes I've seen made time and again.

Avoid making this too heady of an endeavor. It need not be extravagant or overly embellished. Make the process easy. Stick to your intentions (think what outcomes you are going for). Pair that effort with an eye on your interests (what makes you engaged).

Simple statements like, *"to be a good person"* or, *"to be a good father"* are clear and to the point. They are also powerful.

Be mindful. Do not rush through an exercise to check off a box. Take some time. If you can quickly write down a purpose statement, that's a start. No matter what you come up with, let it sit with you for at least a day or two before you decide to put it on your map. You can take longer than that if you desire. Hell, you may edit your purpose statement several times, and that's perfectly okay. It takes time to find a purpose statement that fits like a glove.

Do not force this part of your map. If the time doesn't feel right to define your purpose, don't. I didn't find my first statement until I was almost 40. I didn't find the purpose statement I use today until I was in my early fifties. I tend to do things very quickly, but I simply let it come to me in this case. In a way, it found me. I just needed to stay aware and curious.

> Simple purpose statements like, "to be a good person" or, "to be a good father" are clear, to the point, powerful.

READY, SET, NEXT...

To do something on purpose means to do something intentionally. Now that you know your purpose, your work should shift to living in alignment with it. Your purpose statement will help you with this. Keep in mind that this practice will increase your optimism, improve your focus and health, and build resilience. Take note of these related growths and benefits.

Also, don't forget to play with assigning a purpose to the smaller parts of life. You may find this helpful in gaining clarity. You may enjoy how it adds deeper meaning to the precious, little moments of your life.

Finally, congratulations are in order! Now that you've formulated a life purpose statement, the heavy lifting work required of you within this book is complete. Let me say again, "You are finished!" You have identified the Soul Salt elements for the first draft of your map!

There are a couple of final activities in the book you'll want to adopt to honor the effort you've exerted. In the next chapter, we'll talk about how to absorb and celebrate your efforts. Take a few deep breaths. Take a nap if you need to. Then get going. Chapter 11 is action-oriented and now that you have a map to live as the expanded version of you, I want to show you what to do with it!

PURPOSE

Write your Purpose Statement below:

_____

_____

_____

_____

_____

CHAPTER 11

Be Profound, Sexy Will Follow

> *When you're an artist, nobody ever tells you or hits you with the magic wand of legitimacy. You have to hit your own head with your own handmade wand.*
>
> —Amanda Palmer, *The Art of Asking*

Being profound doesn't need to be sexy. Being profound is honest ... it is earnest ... it is a descriptor of the hard work you've completed if you've tackled the exercises in this book. And let's be honest, this brand of profundity IS sexy. If you're willing, there's a final Rubicon to cross, one that will leave you feeling profound, powerful, wiser, and a bit sexier (if that's possible). Let's cross!

SHARING WHAT YOU'VE LEARNED

What is this line I'm challenging you to cross, and why? Let's start with the *what*. What I'm asking you to do is declare your own truth to someone else—share who you are and what you can achieve by embracing who you are. I'm challenging you to read all of the information you've plotted on your map to a witness of your choosing. That's the challenge.

It takes a lot of courage to speak your truth. You've been diligent in learning how to stop robbing yourself of joy, possibility, and love. You've crafted your own navigation system to guide you to those three gifts and more. Now, it's time to bear witness to how you can fully live your life from a place of personal truth. You have excavated how to be yourself in the short- and the long-term. You did that. You are the artist and creator of your future and you have a map to guide you. Now it is time to give your work legitimacy.

Dan Cable, Francesca Gino, and Bradley Staats conducted some interesting research during the on-boarding process of new hires. They added a process where new employees wrote for three minutes each about, "when have you been at your very best?" Once complete, they had the new hires share what they wrote with co-workers by reading it out loud. After 6 months, these employees were 32% less likely to quit and were 11% happier compared to the control group. In an industry with a high turnover rate, these were significant numbers.[1] And that gets to the *why* of this challenge.

It takes a lot of courage to speak your truth.

In her TED Talk, sociologist Christina Carter shared how this kind of truth-telling is a requirement if you want to live your best life.[2] First, it is a brain thing. Your brain is designed to need human contact and connection, and that need runs strong and deep. Matthew Lieberman, a Professor and Social Cognitive Neuroscientist, wrote an entire book on the topic titled, *Social: Why Our Brains Are Wired to Connect*. In his book, Lieberman states, "What all mammalian infants, from tree shrews to human babies really need from the moment of birth is a caregiver who is committed to making sure that the infant's biological needs are met. . . . Food, water, and shelter are *not* the most basic needs for an infant. Instead, being socially connected and cared for is paramount."[3]

Sharing such personal information with someone else will not only give you a stronger connection to that person, but to your map and yourself as well. Giving voice to your map also provides a chance to see if it rings true to you. You'll notice the places where the guidance is solid, while also recognizing if something still seems a little hollow. It's a wonderful opportunity to test drive the map in a safe environment. Finally, a certain portion of the population are what we call *external processors*, which means these people organize their thoughts by speaking and thinking out loud.[4] If this description fits, you'll find that this exercise will help you organize, understand, or even clarify the information on your map in an astute and useful manner.

> Giving voice to your map provides a chance to see if it rings true to you. You'll notice the places where the guidance is solid, and recognize if something seems a little hollow.

I hope what I've said thus far has convinced you to share your truth with someone and helped you see that the returns from doing so outweigh any fears and insecurities you may have. And, if you are wondering how to jump in and start sharing about your new life, I've provided some steps that will help you with the process.

PREPARE TO SHARE!

Step One: Consolidate all of the answers you've excavated so far in one place.

- This is a great time to transfer all of your answers to the map in the back of the book, or one that you've printed from my website at www.soulsalt.com/book, if you haven't done so already.

- Remember that your map need not be perfect—it will never be perfect. It only needs to fit the bare-bones condition of *necessary*, by which I mean that there is enough information in each map area for you to at least share one item per section. One item is enough. That's all that is necessary.

- Don't wait to share your map until it feels more complete. See above point.

Step Two: Choose your witness.

- You want a person who is open, willing, and that you trust completely.

- This person is going to listen to you share the contents of your map. Their **only** role is to listen … that's it. They need not comment, and indeed there is no invitation for critique. This person is there to "witness" you hearing yourself as you share the wisdom of your map.

- You may ask them to listen with a supportive expression, curiosity, wonder, compassion, and silence.

- If you're feeling fully supported, you could ask, "From your vantage point, did I miss anything positive or important?"

Step Three: Share your map.

- Feel free to make any edits or additions you feel would benefit the evolution of your map.

Step Four: Reflect on these questions:

- What insight did you gain from the experience?
- What happened that felt satisfying?
- What will you change?

That's it! That's the challenge.

WHAT DOES SHARING YOUR MAP LOOK LIKE?

The first time I shared my map, the impact was great. I recognized that I wanted to rename one of my core values. I changed *open-honesty* to *integrity*. That edit felt right-as-rain when I heard myself say the hyphenated title out loud. My heart said, "That means integrity, Lyn. *Use integrity as your word.*" I also understood the gravity of my belief in karma—one of my unshakable truths—which I had not given enough respect.

The second time I shared my map was with the SoulSalt Inc. team. I felt totally supported so I asked for their feedback and discovered I was missing one of my greatest strengths—innovation. I can't believe this word was missing from my map, particularly since *innovation* has been in the title of my last three corporate roles. Without my team as a witness, I might still be missing this vital acknowledgement of a superpower.

Another example of what it's like to share your map comes from my client Brooke Stencil, an executive who I've been nurturing for advancement. She read her map to her husband and shared the following experience with me:

> I remember taking my laptop into his home office and reading my leadership map. Sharing things like my philosophy, aspirations, beliefs, etc. It's interesting being vulnerable like that with your spouse because, in part, a lot of what's baked into the leadership map is aspirational (outside of the aspirations themselves). It's who I feel I am and who I am on my best day.

161

Sharing this with someone who knows me probably better than anyone on the planet, who has surely seen me at my best and my worst, was a vulnerable experience! Fortunately, because he knows me well, he gave me lots of encouragement and positive feedback on what I'd written. He validated the areas that felt really spot on with who I am and even who I want to be and added some ideas for how to make it even better. I felt seen and uplifted. I felt like I knew myself a bit better and as someone who wants to continuously evolve and become a better person, I felt it gave me a good sense of who I am and what makes me.

Your sharing experience will be unique as no two maps are the same. However, there are a few tips and cautionary tales for every reader to note.

TIPS AND CAUTIONS

Let's review a few tips for sharing and some misdirected notions that might knock you off track. I'd hate for that to happen during this vulnerable assignment. And, since these are quite common, they might.

Don't rob yourself of this profound *aha* moment. The first thing to know is that this step is one you don't want to ignore. In other words, fail to read your map out loud and you are robbing yourself of a huge payout. No one can tell you what it will be, but it will cost you something for sure.

Be conscientious of who you ask to be your witness. This person must have demonstrated their trustworthiness to you. They need to have your best interests in mind and at heart. Their intent should be to give you the best of their attention.

Don't let fear or anxiety win. If you're thinking that you are too shy, or the information is too personal to share, think again. Yes this information is personal, and even more so, it is potent and powerful.

Which means it's even more crucial that you muster the courage to share. Yes, you will test yourself, but that will ultimately reward you with an increase in confidence.

Am I challenging you to grow? You bet! Have you done hard things already in this process? Hell yes. Can you do this hard thing now? Yes, yes you can! Do it for yourself. Do it for your growth. Do it so you can look yourself in the eye and claim the bragging rights of speaking your truth out loud. Clinical psychologist Carla Marie Manly asserts that when we express ourselves out loud, we become more aware of what is going on in our mind. We also access the brain's language center and become more intentional.[5] Carla Marie and I give you permission to kick that naysayer out the door.

Finally, I know that reading out loud is a generally dreaded activity for many. Remember Lo? After reading her map out loud to her partner, she reported to me, "You know Lyn, we don't get encouraged very often to read things out loud when we're adults. When we are small and learning to read, out loud is the way to go. Later on in life it is more appropriate and accepted to read silently in our heads. But reading my map out loud gave me insights I could not have gained otherwise."

Go ahead, break the taboo—read it out loud.

A STORY FROM HALLMARK ABOUT SHARING YOUR TRUTH

In his book, *Orbiting the Giant Hairball*, Gordon McKenzie shared a story of presenting an inventive philosophy to Hallmark management. Known as the "holy man" of Hallmark for his artwork in their greeting cards, McKenzie used his gift of disarming foolishness as he shared his ideas before upper management.

He opened his remarks by confessing that he was not qualified to discourse on the profound subject of corporate organization. He proceeded to stand behind the podium, shave off his beard, and introduce a guest speaker to pontificate for him. After shaving and donning a business shirt and tie, he concluded the introduction, "Please join me in welcoming Dr. Sheldon Watts."

He began to clap and gesture toward the back of the room. Everyone in the room turned in their chairs and began to applaud. This gave Gordon the perfect moment to duck behind the podium to put on a wig and horn-rimmed glasses.

"Thank you! Thank you!" the exuberant Dr. Watts exclaimed as the disguised Gordon reappeared behind the mic. He went on to give his dissertation. He shared his truth. Upon his final remarks, the audience burst into an electrified standing ovation.

While the speech didn't ultimately change how Hallmark operates, it had a liberating effect on McKenzie. He convinced himself that his cardinal path was to assist anyone who longed for a fuller, more original work experience. This path is one he said brought him both adventure and soulful richness.[6]

Once you share your truth as Gordon did, you are primed to head down your own cardinal path. Your map will be the best tool you can have by your side. Sharing it will not only make you stronger, but also ready ... ready for the final step. The final step for you to take is this: *once you know your truth, live it!* In the next chapter we'll explore just how you want to go about doing that.

CHAPTER 12

Full Throttle Into Your Future

I wish I had $100 for every time I, or one of my clients said something like, "I knew what to do … I just didn't do it." We can have all the knowledge in the world, but the *knowing* nets us nothing. It's putting that knowledge into action that moves mountains and changes lives.

Some might think that because they've done so much work to get to this point, they're finished with the process. They feel they have gained enough value from the exercises and can just keep these things in mind … and that will be good. While there is great value in crafting the map, I'm convinced that the greatest benefits come from actually living it.

After making it this far and completing my challenging exercises, I bet you don't want to settle in any aspect of your life. You want to use all of the information you've excavated and you want that information to be life-altering.

It's easy for me to say, "Now follow the guidance of your map and go live your best life." But it wouldn't be fair for me to say that without providing some last bit of coaching around how to be successful in doing that. This chapter will ensure you know how to use the map you just created. It may seem obvious to some, and overwhelming to others. So, let me show you how to move at full throttle into your future, regardless of your level of comfort.

> We can have all the knowledge in the world, but the knowing nets us nothing. It's putting that knowledge into action that moves mountains and changes lives.

There are two simple practices I will show you to remove the burden if this seems daunting and that will add confidence, even if you already know what to do.

The first is to focus on embodying your map. I use the word *embodiment* with purpose because it means you give tangible form to each aspect of your map. In short, what someone sees on your map is what they see reflected in your actions and words.

The second is formulating your own schedule to consistently review your map and make revisions. You are not the same person now that you were before you started working through this book. I imagine that in six months, if you have deliberately used your map, you will have evolved even more. So, let's take a look at part one and learn how to embody the work you've done so far.

PART ONE - MAKING YOUR MAP REAL FOR YOU

Embodiment is the process of activating items on your map into your day-to-day actions. It flows through your decisions, thoughts, and emotions. But this doesn't happen without effort. This is indeed where things get real and the items on your map become tangible. If they haven't yet, the people around you will see a visible representation of your map in the form of how you live your life.

The following steps will guide you to embody your map:

Step One: Make the conscious choice to use your map as a continuous guide. This means finding a mirror, looking yourself in the eye, and telling yourself you intend to use this map from this point forward to guide you through life. And, tell yourself *why* you want to do this.

The neuroscientist Andrew Huberman calls this having a "reason kit." What are your relevant reasons for investing the time and effort into making your map come alive? Here is a depiction of mine:

You might know your reasons already. But if you don't, this short list of motivating factors may spark some thoughts. It's curated from years of noticing what clients use in their reason kits.

Autonomy	Professionalism	Results-Oriented
Mastery	Honesty	Independence
Peace of Mind	Truth	Be Excited
Self-Efficacy	Sick & Tired	Act
Beauty	Achievement	Prove to Myself
Rightness	Get Paid	Create
Change	Make a Shift	Be Discovered

Be My Best Self	Increase Justice	Safety
Learning	Shine a Light	Sanity
Make Space	Share	Strength
Research	Being Accepted	Progress
Support Others	Inner Peace	Purpose
Transformation	Personal Growth	Victory
Connection	Freedom	Success
Focus	Adventure	Inspiration
Loyalty	Passion	Harmony
Advocacy	Contentment	Being Generous
Integrity	Meaning	Discovery
Take a Risk	Self-Efficacy	Get Recognition
Establish Myself	Life Leadership	Problem-Solve
Prove Something	Satisfaction	Add Value
Invent	Valor	Satisfy Curiosity
Advancement	Love	Build Trust
Fairness	Be Generative	Fulfillment
Responsibility	Challenge-Taker	High Quality

Below are some examples of what you might tell yourself while looking in the mirror:

> *I intend to use my map like a guide. It will help me make both critical choices and small decisions. I see myself referring to it weekly and recording my thoughts and progress at least twice a week. My reason for taking this action is that I value and believe strongly that personal improvement is one of the most important functions of my life. It is one of my values.*

> *My map is my most trusted resource. I reflect upon it monthly and will discuss my practice of utilizing it with my coach on*

a bi-monthly basis. I want this map to inject who I am into every single part of my life. I'll know I'm successful if each yearly review I hold with myself leaves me feeling great. I use it to be more authentic and satisfied than I was before I had my map.

I want to be my best self. I can't want that and not have a way to get there. My reasons for living what I put on my map are pretty simple. I just want to do and be my best as much as possible.

If you have some reasons ready to put in your kit, list 3-5 of them here:

_____

_____

_____

Step Two: Pick one or two aspects of your map to focus on at a time, then choose a period of time to practice living in alignment with those elements. I like to call these *practice sessions*. Some people like to designate a whole day for a session. Others may do just a morning or afternoon, while still others may specify just an hour or two, here or there. Think about what works best for you and add the time slots to your schedule.

Aspects of the map to focus on:

_____

_____

Time periods to practice these aspects:

_____

_____

Here are a couple of example sessions that I created for myself:

> *I keep my map visible. It sits above the monitor of my computer. I deliberately activate a single section of my map every other day. Meaning that on Monday I might work to align with my core values. On Wednesday I may focus on using one or two of my main strengths. By Friday I could be looking over the week to determine if I met my metric for success this week. I'd also, at that time, set into play my intention to have a successful weekend.*
>
> *Every week I hold a wrap-up session with myself. I like to do this on Sunday mornings over a cup of coffee before my partner wakes up. I review my map and make a few notes in my journal about what went well and what impact my map had on my life (both professional and personally). I do not plan ahead. Instead, I read my map each Saturday and that keeps it fresh in my mind. By the next Saturday, I always have two to five examples of how it has guided me.*

Create your own sessions and schedule when you're going to practice activating your map. The idea is to be consistent. Set an intention to get at least two, if not more, deliberate moments during the week.

Step Three: Reflect. Think, write about, and discuss the experiences you've had with your map each week.

Use a notebook or digital media to reflect and write about your experience. Former olympic champion Lanny Bassham, in his quest to become a champion, learned how the top athletes succeed. Every single one reflected and wrote about their practice sessions. When you reflect, feel free to use Lanny's three questions as your prompts:

1. *What insight or learning did I gain?*
2. *What went well?*
3. *What will I do next time?*

Step Four: Rest. Don't keep pushing and forcing yourself to practice. Do the work and then rest.

Research shows that neuro-connections (learning or neuroplasticity) gained from an activity that we've intently focused on hardwire during rest? That's right, the new neuro-network connection is actually strengthened during rest, *not* during the activity.

Example:

I work on my map about three times a week. I keep a brightly colored binder on my desk. Inside, I have placed my map and created tabs for each month of the year. I record my efforts right after activating some portion of my map. For instance, today I met up with my daughter for lunch. One of the items on my beliefs/philosophy section is to make regular contact with my child. After meeting with Liz, I wrote about how meeting with her and connecting to her ticked the box on this part of my map. Yesterday I caught myself using my strength of inspiration with my work team. I rallied them in a sales meeting and told them how much they mean to me. I acknowledged each individual with a sincere pat on the back for a specific effort they had recently made. It felt great to use that muscle and see how it helped us all be better. I don't know if I'll add any more entries in my binder this week. I might let my mind rest a bit, but be sure about this, next week I'll be making two or three more entries. That's just how I roll.

I love to use Lanny's three questions as I reflectively write about my practice sessions. I can see that over a period of three months, I'm more conscious about both my words and actions. I know for sure that writing out my thoughts as frequently as possible has been the reason for this.

Step Five: Repeat. Generate as many high-quality repetitions of these four steps as you feel is good. Consider your circadian rhythm, or the time of day when you feel most focused. These hours would be ideal for practice times.

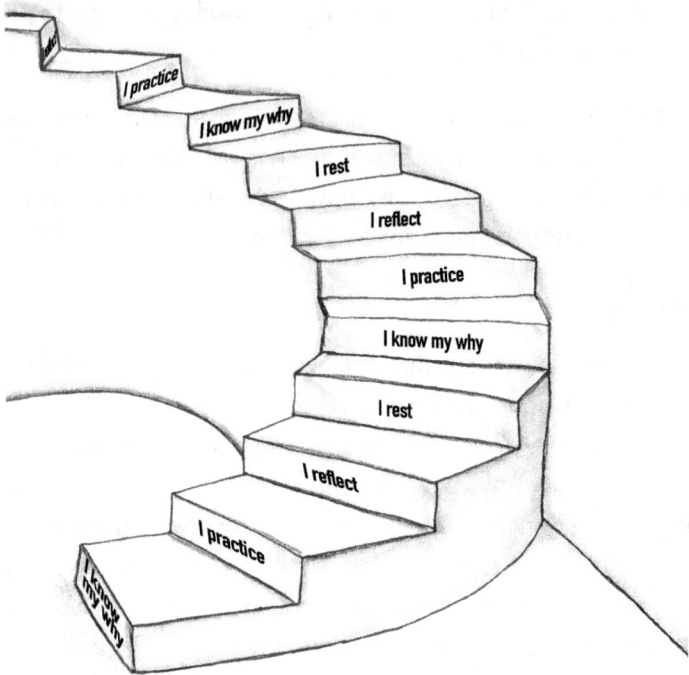

Examples of more flexible practice sessions:

I'm a morning person. If I don't focus on some aspect of my map between 9 a.m. and 1:00 p.m, I don't have the energy to give it that it deserves.

I am a bit of a night owl. My most productive time is generally from 4:00 p.m. to 10:00 p.m. and that is when I work on parts of my map. I write a value, or a belief, or a strength on a sticky note three to four times a week. I keep these in front of me right after my afternoon coffee. That way some part of my map is front-of-mind.

I don't like to pre-plan how to implement the things listed on my map. Instead, I notice when I'm living part of my map, then pull out my phone and write a quick note about the experience. If I can get two items noted per week, and if I can review my map once a month, I feel like I'm giving it the appropriate amount of attention.

Now it's your turn. How will you schedule practice time? How do you sense you can best embody your map?

Write how you will keep practicing aspects of your map on a regular interval below:

_____

_____

_____

PART TWO – REVIEW AND REVISE

Your map is healthier, more vital, and more vibrant when it is allowed to evolve. Let it be as dynamic as you are. The following steps are a proven method for allowing it to evolve. See if you can come up with your own revision calendar.

Step One: Determine how often do you think you'd like to revise and edit your map. Like me, most of my clients tend to revise more frequently when the map is new. Over time, you'll probably find that twice a year, or quarterly, or even annually is enough. Hell, there have been times when I didn't edit and revise my map for a period of two years!

> *Your map is healthier, more vital, and more vibrant when it is allowed to evolve. Let it be as dynamic as you are.*

While you're contemplating your time period, consider these comments from other map makers:

> *"I like to review and revise my map twice a year. Our company is so dynamic and my role in Product Management is a*

constant of change. I find that if I review and revise twice a year, I feel more confident that I'm up to date with myself. This frequency helps me to dip and jive with the influx of products moving through our company."

"Once a year I rent a room either in a hotel or cabin or the like. I generally leave on a Friday night and return home by Saturday afternoon. I don't go far because this time is for me to have quiet meals, restful sleep, and space to completely review my map. It isn't about traveling very far."

"Sometimes I make major changes to the map. I celebrate my growth and advancement in understanding who I am and how to get the best out of myself. Other years I find I don't need to do much. Maybe I make a few tweaks and I'm good to go. Staying committed to this sort of practice has given me freedom to ask myself hard questions. It has given me confidence that I know who I am, and I know how I'm growing. I look forward to this annual, personal retreat. It is one of the most empowering practices I have in my life."

Step Two: After you have decided how often to revise, return to the exercise of reading your map out loud. Every revised version of your map deserves a chance to be heard and witnessed. So, pick your safe person, pick your time, and read it out loud. It might surprise you how reading it out loud again helps you notice adjustments that you want to make. You may hear it all flow so well that you nailed the revision the first time through. There's no right or wrong, good or bad here, only the process of revising, re-reading, and seeing what happens for you.

Step Three: Schedule your next revision session now. Put it on your calendar and honor that date.

Step Four: Repeat and enjoy!

AVOID THESE MISGUIDED BELIEFS

I wouldn't be a very good coach if I didn't warn you about some of the misguided beliefs that often pop up at this time in the process. I've seen them many times with my clients, keep the following in mind:

Don't think the process you've just completed is a one-and-done proposition. Sometimes people think that since they've done all the exercises in the book, they don't need to review or revise. If that belief pops up, just go back and read the very first section of this chapter again. You don't want to sit idle with this knowledge. When no action is taken, no results happen!

Don't act like anything less than the CEO of your life. No successful business attempts to function without some sort of strategic planning. Consider that putting things on paper makes the commitment to yourself more tangible and increases the possibility that you will succeed. The American Society for Training and Development[1] put forth these research data points:

The probability of completing a goal is:

- 10% if you hear an idea
- 25% if you consciously decide to adopt it.
- 40% if you decide when you will do it.
- 50 % if you plan how you will do it.
- 65% if you commit to someone else you will do it.
- 95% if you have a specific accountability appointment with the person to whom you committed.

If you want to lead your life like a strong CEO, do some strategic planning and set intentions and goals. Do it regularly and include commitments to yourself, witnessed by other people, to increase your chance of success.

Don't get bogged down by overdoing it with your map. There are no Soul Salt Olympics. So, take a rest once you've built your map, if you need a rest. However, when you're ready, these three things are scientifically proven to be powerful elements of personal growth and neuroplasticity:

- Be willing to improve.
- Be willing to change.
- Be willing to expand.

When you embody these three concepts, you can embody your map quickly and reap great benefits.

When no action is taken, no results happen!

Don't think having a reason to implement your map isn't important. Simply wanting to implement is not enough. You may not fully believe in the *reason kit* yet. Fair enough. However, consider that when you place a reason behind living in alignment with your map (or any other venture), you promote automatic arousal in your system and release epinephrine, which is your brain's version of adrenalin. You actually ignite the power of your own neurochemicals when you have a reason backing your action. So, give it a try and you discover the reason kit is more useful than you expected.

Don't try to live all of your map, all of the time. Breaking practices and embodiment sessions into smaller chunks is not pointless. Not only do we have circadian rhythms at play in our neurobiology, we also have ultradian patterns, which means that within any given 24-hour period most of us can only focus for about 90 minutes at a time with what might be labeled as *deep focus*. Even within a deeply focused period of 90 minutes there is a bell curve. We start out warming up our capacity to focus, then we reach a peak, and then focus diminishes until our powers are worn and need a break.

CONFIDENCE, PURPOSE, AND FULFILLMENT

You've done the work and now should feel proud and empowered that you can live an extraordinary life. Putting your map to use is the only way to honor your effort and the amazing person you've discovered (or rediscovered). You should have confidence after this chapter about how to make sure you get ongoing value from your map instead of considering this the end of the journey. Make a commitment to yourself that you will utilize the two activities I provided to maximize your discoveries—practice and review.

You ignite the power of your own neurochemicals when you have a reason backing your action.

Practice makes progress. As I mentioned in the beginning of this chapter, if you don't take action on something you will not yield any results. The first action to take is to understand your reasons and your why. When you look yourself in the eye and voice these things aloud, you will begin to embody your map. Then, put the elements on your map into practice by focusing on a couple elements at a time, for short periods, or sessions. This will help you make progress to where you want go, and help you better refine your map to be the best guide for navigating life. Don't panic if your map needs to change. It will transform along with you as you evolve and grow through life—as long as you are putting it to practice.

Review allows you to revise. Your goal isn't to get your map perfect out of the gate. It won't be, so don't put that pressure on yourself. Your goal is to learn, through practice, where your map may need to be tweaked. As you practice the elements of your map and embody your true self more and more, you will outgrow some elements and may need to find new ones that fit better. It's kind of like a child's clothes after a growth spurt—they no longer fit and need to be updated. When you update your map regularly, the guidance stays authentic to the ever-expanding version of who you are, and allows you to operate from the current vision of who you want to be. Pick a time period that makes sense for reviewing your map and honor yourself, and your map, with regular check-ins. You'll thank me later. Mostly, you'll thank yourself!

Your goal isn't to get your map perfect out of the gate. It won't be, so don't put that pressure on yourself.

I'm extremely proud of the accomplishment you've made by finishing this book and the exercises in it. Living in alignment with the salt of your soul is truly the map to confidence, purpose, and fulfillment. I'm so excited for the possibilities your future holds! Stick with it. You can do it. I promise, if you use your map the way I've coached you, you'll feel the change and the control you have over your life that you probably only dreamed would be possible.

And remember, I am here to support and encourage you as well. Just because we're to the end of the book does not mean we have to say goodbye. If you'd like to continue our relationship, I'd love to share a few ways we can continue to bless each other's lives:

- Visit www.soulsalt.com to read more of Lyn's writing and to learn about our products and services.

- If you are interested in having Lyn speak at an upcoming event, or to your team, please email info@soulsalt.com.

- Connect on Social Media:

    Facebook - www.facebook.com/soulsaltinc

    Instagram - www.instagram.com/soulsaltinc

    LinkedIn - www.linkedin.com/company/soulsalt-inc

ACKNOWLEDGEMENTS

Last Words and Salutations

I n my life, like yours, there are individuals who contribute uniquely, who make a meaningful impact and never know it. I say this because I have learned something valuable from almost every encounter I've ever had. That is why I find it impossible to recognize each and every person who has taught, guided, inspired, supported, or encouraged me along the way. Know, if you and I have spent time together prior to publishing this book, a part of you has influenced it in some way. To you all, I say thank you.

Let me now specifically recognize those who made a direct influence upon this project:

Language fails me in converting the gratitude I have for Susan McLaughlin and her undying support. While I spent weekends and evenings on this project, she never once complained. In fact, her encouragement got me through a few dark moments and several weary afternoons. Thank you Susan!

To the children in my life and their partners, spouses, and littles, thank you for putting up with me and my many pivots. I appreciate and respect you for loving me and enduring all the moments when

I could not stop talking about my work and this book, or what I was doing next on this project. You've seen me through a few transformations and loved me no matter what. That gift has been life sustaining. And you know I mean that literally. So, I say thank you to Derrek, Ainsley, Megan, Chase, Jessica, Elsie, Eddy and Baby Wilson.

To the members of our very own SoulSalt Writer's Room (because I couldn't get the first version of this book out of my soul without your help) I say PHEW! Thank you, thank you for the hours and weeks you labored with me to translate the SoulSalt coaching process out in the open and on paper. Janie Gabbett, your expertise with writing and editing was the anchor and foundation we all needed. Penny Frates, the clever way you say things and the depth to which you know me, and my coaching process was validating and inspiring. Jessica Draper, your willingness to add your vantage point and pound out some vital concepts in the first manuscript made it possible to keep the momentum going. Chloe Riley, can I say "wow!" Your presence and writing made Jennifer Nash's Author Accelerator incubator doable. And Jennifer, thank you for taking my book on. Your coaching moved the manuscript to a place where we could find a publisher.

Which brings me to Kevin and Stephanie Mullani. Kevin, your expertise as a publisher is outstanding. Your guidance, patience, and your wisdom have taken a manuscript and made it exceptional. Thank you for introducing us to Stephanie so that we could leverage her artistry and expertise. Erin and I benefited from both of you giving us creative direction.

And that brings up you Erin Blutt. From the moment I saw your doodles I knew we could understand each other on a level that other people often miss. From stickers, to magnets, to illustrating this book, I've been a fan of your sketches and creative eye. Thank you for being brave and stepping up when I needed you most.

There's a special thanks to you Shauna. You've been a friend and a confidant. Mostly you've been a cheerleader and a huge support for this project. Without your encouragement and support I'd still be talking about this book instead of sending it out to the world. Just so you know, a bit of that twinkle in your eye is in this book.

Also, a special nod to Andrea Lang. Andrea, you've been an advocate for my work for years. I hold a special place in my heart for your grit, your courage, your business acumen, and your unending connection. Thank you.

Sunni Brown, I hope you know that *Doodle Revolution* changed my life forever. You were the first person to validate my visual thinking attributes. When you acknowledged this part of me I valued it even more dearly. You have been an inspiration. I thank you for opening up so many minds and hearts. The world needs more Sunni Browns. Also, thank you for getting this book and I connected to Jennifer Nash and her incubator.

I want to thank you Jon and Johanna Nastor for being terrific partners in building the buzz and SEO for me and SoulSalt Inc. I have the utmost respect and confidence in your skills. Thank you for partnering with candor and professionalism. I have grown to respect you both and it doesn't hurt that you are terrific human beings.

Cindy Feldman, you always take my work and spread the news. I know you've already connected me to speaking opportunities before the book came out. I know you'll continue be a great promoter of this book. For all you do for us, thank you.

To Shannon Dee, I thank you for holding down the company while all of this writing was storming through our ranks. Without your stealthy scheduling of client sessions, our work would have faltered, and the writing would have waned.

To my Conversational Intelligence© sisters I am indebted. Our retreats in Manhattan and on Lake Oscawana encouraged and accelerate crafting this book. Thank you to Deborah Naish, Deborah (Goldie) Goldstein, and Lisa Hart.

Finally, I have to thank people who will never read this book and yet made it possible for me to keep my voice alive through some tough, tough years. Grandpa Morris and Grandma Ruth, I adore you. Jack and Rachel, thank you for treating me like your own and buying me cowboy boots when I needed to kick up a little shit. And then there is Val, my cousin-brother. I hope this book supports others at critical junctures as you supported me.

List of Core Values

Excitement	Clarity	Patience
Change	Fun-Loving	Self-Respect
Goodness	Charisma	Abundance
Involvement	Humor	Reciprocity
Faith	Leadership	Enjoyment
Wisdom	Renewal	Entrepreneurial
Beauty	Home	Happiness
Caring	Be-True	Harmony
Personal Development	Contentment	Peace
Family	Honesty	Courage
Freedom	Adventure	Balance
Security	Kindness	Compassion
Loyalty	Teamwork	Fitness
Intelligence	Career	Professionalism
Connection	Communication	Relationship

Creativity	Learning	Knowledge
Humanity	Excellence	Patience
Success	Innovation	Change
Respect	Quality	Prosperity
Invention	Commonality	Wellness
Diversity	Contributing	Finances
Generosity	Spiritualism	Gratitude
Integrity	Strength	Grace
Finesse	Entertain	Endurance
Love	Wealth	Facilitation
Openness	Speed	Effectiveness
Religion	Power	Fun
Order	Affection	Fame
Advancement	Cooperation	Justice
Friendship	Love of Career	Appreciation
Joy / Play	Friendship / Relationship	Willingness
Forgiveness	Encouragement	Trusting your Gut
Work Smarter	Pride in Your Work	Giving People a Chance
This Too Shall Pass Attitude		

Your Map!

The following two pages contain your personal map. You can add the answers you generate as you go through the exercises in this book, or all at once at the end. Because space is limited, you will have to choose "keywords" to represent your answers in some cases.

Fill out the map here and carry this book around to ensure decisions are in line with your true self. Or, download a printable version of the map at www.soulsalt.com/book. Or, do both!

Have fun and congratulations again for finishing the work in this book!

VALUES

_____
_____
_____

UPNs

_____
_____

INSPIRATION

_____
_____

SUCCESS

_____
_____

CAUTION ZONE

_____
_____
_____

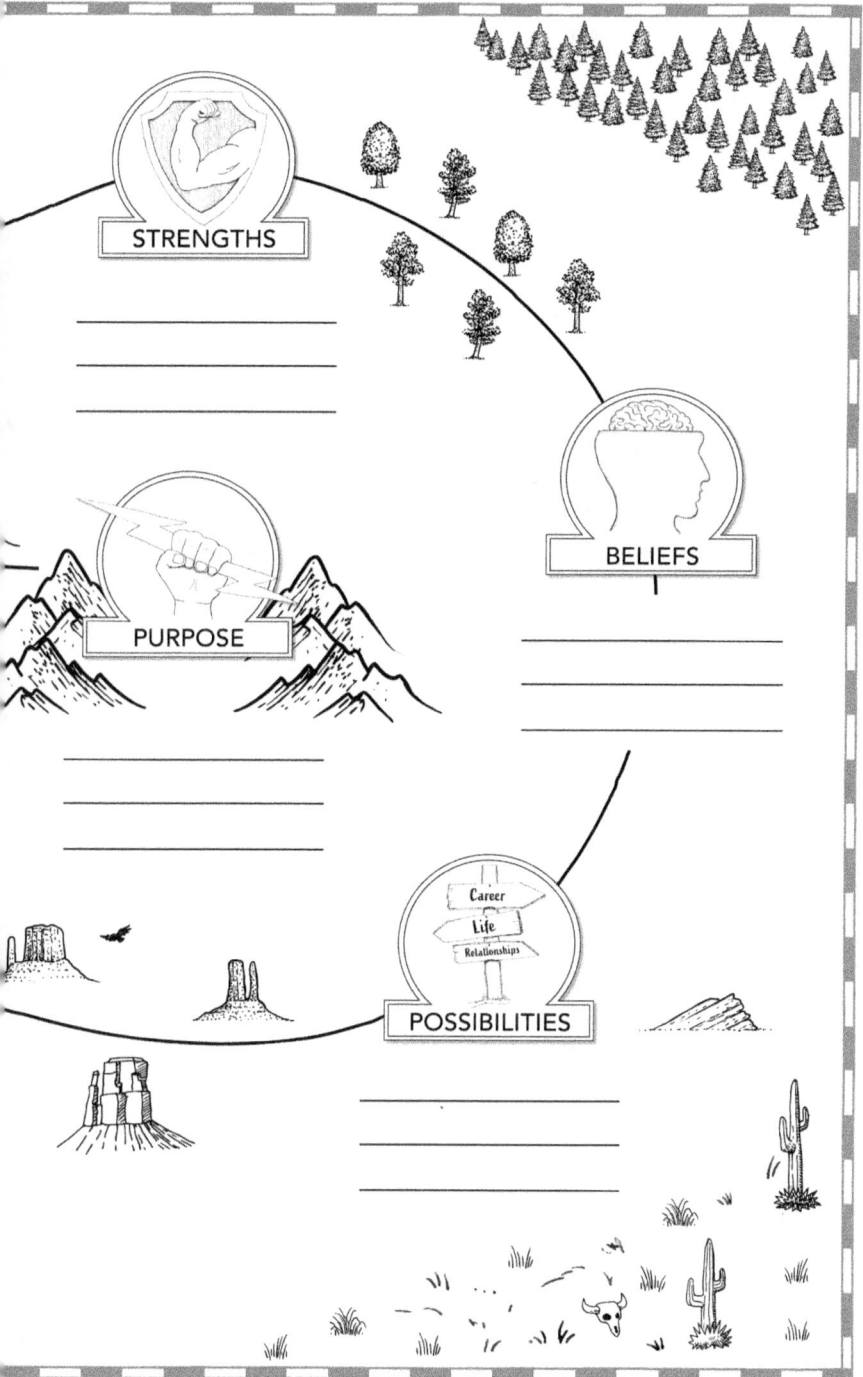

STRENGTHS

_____
_____
_____

PURPOSE

_____
_____
_____

BELIEFS

_____
_____

POSSIBILITIES

Career
Life
Relationships

_____
_____
_____

END NOTES

INTRODUCTION

1. https://bronnieware.com/regrets-of-the-dying/

2. https://www.youtube.com/watch?v=_wby302sRFU

3. https://www.manoa.hawaii.edu/exploringourfluidearth/chemical/chemistry-and-seawater/salty-sea/weird-science-salt-essential-life

4. https://www.manoa.hawaii.edu/exploringourfluidearth/chemical/chemistry-and-seawater/salty-sea/weird-science-salt-essential-life

5. https://www.npr.org/sections/13.7/2014/11/08/362478685/from-salt-to-salary-linguists-take-a-page-from-science

6. https://www.phrases.org.uk/meanings/worth-ones-salt.html

CHAPTER 1

1. https://dreammakerr.com/life-coaching-statistics/#Key_Life_Coaching_Statistics

2. https://dreammakerr.com/life-coaching-statistics/#Key_Life_Coaching_Statistics

3. https://coachingfederation.org/research/global-coaching-study

4. https://researchportal.coachfederation.org/Document/Pdf/2968.pdf

5. https://researchportal.coachfederation.org/Document/Pdf/abstract_190

6. https://www.jmir.org/2021/7/e27774

7. https://researchportal.coachfederation.org/Document/Pdf/abstract_190

8. https://researchportal.coachfederation.org/Document/Pdf/abstract_190

9. https://radar.brookes.ac.uk/radar/file/2d76c41c-6628-4eed-8a8a-4d0a5c4f5540/1/special11-paper-05.pdf

10. https://marshallgoldsmith.com/meet-marshall/

11. https://www.fairwayresolution.com/resources/whats-new/mbit—-using-your-multiple-brains

12. https://www.harleytherapy.co.uk/counselling/reach-your-full-potential.htm

13. https://www.zippia.com/advice/career-change-statistics/

CHAPTER 2

1. https://www.frontiersin.org/articles/10.3389/fphys.2019.00509/full

2. https://pubmed.ncbi.nlm.nih.gov/31728781/#:~:text=Recent%20findings%3A%20Dr.,has%20its%20own%20nervous%20system

3. mBraining: Using your Multiple Brains to do Cool Stuff, Grant Soosalu and Marvin Oka, 2012

4. mBraining: Using your Multiple Brains to do Cool Stuff, Grant Soosalu and Marvin Oka, 2012

5. mBraining: Using your Multiple Brains to do Cool Stuff, Grant Soosalu and Marvin Oka, 2012

6. mBraining: Using your Multiple Brains to do Cool Stuff, Grant Soosalu and Marvin Oka, 2012

7. https://www.theguardian.com/science/blog/2012/feb/28/how-many-neurons-human-brain

8. https://www.brainfacts.org/in-the-lab/meet-the-researcher/2018/how-many-neurons-are-in-the-brain-120418#:~:text=For%20half%20a%20century%2C%20neuroscientists,a%20different%20number%20—%2086%20billion

9. https://today.uconn.edu/2018/08/know-thyself-philosophy-self-knowledge/

CHAPTER 3

1. https://www.psychologicalscience.org/observer/the-heart-of-the-matter

2. https://gmatjumpstart.com/gmat-study-plan/

CHAPTER 4

1. https://medlineplus.gov/ency/article/000013.htm

2. https://www.medicalnewstoday.com/articles/325174#:~:text=As%20a%20general%20rule%20of,age

3. https://pubmed.ncbi.nlm.nih.gov/20069776/

4. https://www.cnvc.org/training/resource/needs-inventory

CHAPTER 5

1. https://hbr.org/2009/02/stop-overdoing-your-strengths

2. https://www.gallup.com/cliftonstrengths/en/266435/
   unleash-people-strengths-help-manage-weaknesses.aspx

3. https://hbr.org/2009/02/stop-overdoing-your-strengths

4. https://positivepsychology.com/self-knowledge/

CHAPTER 6

1. https://medium.com/@NataliMorad/how-to-be-an-adult-
   kegans-theory-of-adult-development-
   d63f4311b553#:~:text=Stage%204%20—%20The%20
   Self%20Authoring,adults%20live%20at%20this%20
   stage.&text=In%20Stage%204%2C%20we%20
   can,our%20relationships%20or%20the%20environment

2. https://medium.com/@NataliMorad/how-to-be-an-adult-
   kegans-theory-of-adult-development-
   d63f4311b553#:~:text=Stage%204%20—%20The%20
   Self%20Authoring,adults%20live%20at%20this%20
   stage.&text=In%20Stage%204%2C%20we%20
   can,our%20relationships%20or%20the%20environment

3. https://journals.sagepub.com/doi/
   full/10.1177/0956797616671327

CHAPTER 7

1. https://www.makeawish.org.nz/wishes/the-wish-effect/

2. https://cpb-us-w2.wpmucdn.com/sites.udel.edu/dist/6/132/
   files/2010/11/Psychological-Science-2014-Mueller-
   0956797614524581-1u0h0yu.pdf

3. https://www.topeducationdegrees.org/proven-reasons-to-write-by-hand/

4. https://brainworldmagazine.com/give-your-brain-hopes-and-dreams/

CHAPTER 9

1. https://www.npr.org/sections/health-shots/2020/04/11/815573198/how-stories-connect-and-persuade-us-unleashing-the-brain-power-of-narrative#:~:text=aywan88%2FGetty%20Images-,When%20you%20listen%20to%20a%20story%2C%20your%20brain%20waves%20actually,and%20perspective%2C%20research%20has%20found

2. https://www.harvardbusiness.org/what-makes-storytelling-so-effective-for-learning/#:~:text=Telling%20stories%20is%20one%20of,and%20values%20that%20unite%20people

3. https://www.psu.edu/news/research/story/viewing-memes-online-increases-positive-emotions-helps-cope-pandemic/

CHAPTER 10

1. https://people.ict.usc.edu/~gordon/publications/ACS18.PDF

2. https://www.all-about-psychology.com/the-importance-of-meaning-in-life.html

3. https://www.scottsdalecc.edu/news/2019/why-having-sense-purpose-important#:~:text=Think%20about%20this%3A%20When%20you,Better%20physical%20health

CHAPTER 11

1. http://static1.squarespace.com/
   static/55dcde36e4b0df55a96ab220/t/55e5f041e4b06f3c4b
   89a71b/1441132609616/Cable+Gino+Staats+ASQ+2013.
   pdf

2. https://www.ted.com/talks/christine_carter_the_1_minute_
   secret_to_forming_a_new_habit

3. Social: Why Our Brains Are Wired to Connect, Matthew
   Lieberman, 2014

4. https://www.secondstorycounseling.com/blog/2021/08/
   internal-versus-external-processing

5. https://medium.com/illumination/the-power-of-saying-
   things-out-loud-c82daa49330a

6. Orbiting the Giant Hairball, Gordon McKenzie, 1998

CHAPTER 12

1. https://www.td.org/insights/astd-announces-name-change